REFLECTIONS

Inspirational Stories
from Everyday Life

DARLIS SAILORS

Published by BookLocker.com, Inc., St. Petersburg, Florida, U.S.A.

Printed on acid-free paper.

These inspirational stories are creative nonfiction based on actual events.

BookLocker.com, Inc.
2016

First Edition

This book can be ordered from the publisher, BookLocker.com, or from your favorite online or neighborhood bookstore.

SCRIPTURE REFERENCES

Most of the Scripture texts are from The New International Version (NIV):

Other Scripture sources are designated as:
- (AMP) The Amplified Bible
- (KJV) The King James Version
- (MSG) The Message Bible
- (NAS) The New American Standard
- (NLT) The New Living Translation

To God, The Great Creator,
Who answered prayers for seeds of creative thought

To my husband
Who encouraged me to share my writing

To my brother and his wife
Who believed in me and sponsored this first edition

To my email readers
Who inspired me to send a weekly story

To trusted lifetime friends
Who challenged me with high standards as editors

TABLE OF CONTENTS

POEMS

CHAPTER ONE

CLOSE TO HOME

ABOVE AVERAGE

It is said that the average person moves eleven times in his lifespan. Considering our transient culture, I'm guessing the "above average" category has a major membership. I got a head start on it while growing up in a Midwest minister's home. We moved about every five years until Dad got a call to the Southwest. He and Mom stayed in place there for over twenty years, but I moved on to college and got married.

When I met my husband, he was way "below average." He had lived in the same house his whole life. I was so impressed. What would it be like to live in the same house in the same town all your life? I had already moved six times by the age of sixteen.

When we married, my husband and I planned on working career jobs while doing church volunteer ministries. God allowed us to start that way and in our first three years of married life we lived in two different apartments, one small duplex, a church parsonage and a small house.

For the next twenty-five years we worked in full-time ministry as associate pastors. Sometimes housing was provided. Other times we had to find our own.

We lived in five church parsonages. Two were located next to the church, which created non-privacy issues. We also experienced thin walls and noisy neighbors in two duplexes, limited parking in three condos, and the joys and expenses of ownership while in four single-family homes.

Even while ministering for twelve years as pastors in one church, we made three moves. We started with the parsonage, a mobile home next to the church, but my dream was to have my own home. In that community, affordable pit-set mobiles outnumbered stick-built homes. We left the parsonage and moved two more times before retirement, each time to a pit-set mobile.

My husband might have been "below average" on total moves made while growing up, but he was definitely "above average" in flexibility. His resilience when called upon to move always amazed me.

A friend once gave us a plaque that said, "Blessed are the flexible, for they shall not be broken." Life is not stationary; it moves from infancy to retirement, from kindergarten to college, from single life to becoming a couple, and from job to job. Changes! Blessed are the flexible.

Ecclesiastes 3:1 says, "There is a time for everything." The next eight verses list twenty-eight contrasting activities. To those I would add, "There is a time to move and a time to remain . . . flexible, that is."

GOOD GIFTS

I did not grow up with a dog for a pet. My husband did. But we have had many friends with lovely dogs in a variety of breeds, such as Arthur---a Wheatland Terrier, Sasha---a Shih Tzu, and Sitka---an Alaskan Husky.

We once worked with a pastor who said, "If your dog loves you, don't ask for a second opinion." Pets are a source of comfort and unconditional love that is appreciated by people of every economic level. I know some people abuse their animals and it's hard to stomach stories of blatant mistreatment, but I'm thankful for agencies who do their best as rescuers.

Arthur was a rescue dog. He became trained and certified to make weekly visits to a Veteran's Home. He knew which room to go to and would walk right up to the door and wait. He was self-controlled, patient and very sensitive to each person. When someone passed away, he would not leave until his owner took him into the room patted the empty bed and said, "All gone." Arthur would usually put a paw on the bed or touch it in some way. Then he was ready to go and did not stop at that door again.

Sasha was ready to jump into the car all week long, but our friends said she knew she could not go when they were getting ready for Sunday church. Instead of her usual "let's go" antics, she would settle down quietly into a snugly spot as they left.

Sitka enjoys his igloo-shaped dog house out on the patio, but he does well indoors. My friend is a caregiver for her mother and Sitka has been a comforting companion to them.

She says, "Sitka likes to take me on walks and I've met a lot of neighbors. Sitka is such a people-lover."

When I see the interaction between various kinds of pets and the people who care for them, I think of James 1:17 which says, "Every good and perfect gift is from above, coming down from the Father of the heavenly lights. . ." The Creator of the stars, sun and moon, "saw ALL that He had made, and it was very good" (Genesis 1:31). I'd put pets in that *good* category.

One of the key ingredients in relationships with pets is mutual affection. Happiness flows from us to them and vice versa. I'm glad God made these gifts in such a variety of species, colors and sizes. I always have a little trouble with things labeled *One Size Fits All*.

LETTING GO

To recover from loss of any kind, we must first acknowledge it. We never fully recover if we just "suck it up" and keep going, because emotions don't disappear. They go undercover and come out incognito. For example, resentment may appear as anger, and bitterness as lack of forgiveness.

We need to follow the fisherman's example of catch and release. To catch an emotion is to acknowledge its presence. As long as the fisherman hangs on to his catch, he can tell the same story over and over. It's there and he knows it. But if he wants to have something new, he must release what has already been caught.

When I was a caregiver for my father I had a few emotions to catch and release. I found myself getting angry, then I realized it was caused by resentment. Dad had three children. Why did I have to be the caregiver? My brothers had good reasons for not being involved on a daily basis, but I had to choose to release my negative emotions.

I'm sorry to say that before I became a caregiver I often visited and prayed for the sick, but I don't think I ever gave caregivers much thought. Now when I see them, I think of a phrase from John 15:13 (NAS), "Greater love has no one than this, that one lay down his life for his friends." Caregivers are definitely on my radar now.

After Dad passed away I wrote *Caregiver's Choice*, a poem I believe was part of my grieving process. While Dad was alive my life was not my own, but I made a choice. I refused to be a victim. Psalm 119:45 explains God's Word as my source of victory. It says, "I will walk about in freedom, for I have sought out your precepts."

I hope it's a source of encouragement to others. Letting go of negative emotions may be a caregiver's challenge, but friends and family have a challenge, too. How will you show appreciation to the caregiver closest to you?

CAREGIVER'S CHOICE
By Darlis Sailors

I walk up a hill and sit down on a rock
It's fun to look down like a bird in the air
Who flies where it will in space wide and free

Out here it feels calm, no one to talk or turn up the TV
No one who needs me
I close my eyes and feel at peace
I need this time, I need this space

Up here I feel free, like a bird flying high
With no drag on my wings to stop my flight
I breathe in fresh air and let go of my stress

A break from life, now back I go
Down to the house that feels so small
Back to the one who needs me
I've made a choice—while there, I will freely serve

LOVE LETTERS

A long-time friend once sent an email to ask if I remembered a song called *Love Is Why*? I replied, "Neither my husband nor I remember the words, but maybe you can find them online." I knew she sang solos and thought that was why she had asked.

Weeks later we received a surprising letter, written on the back of a well-worn piece of music. It was dated Sunday, August 7, 1966 and titled *Love Is Why*. My husband had sent this letter to dear college friends shortly after our engagement. They had found it while sorting boxes in preparation for moving.

Many times over the years I had heard my husband say, "I love you," and he had done many good things which proved he meant it. But these words from the past were very special.

He had written, ". . . forgive this letter if it's a little mixed up—you know how it is being in love . . . what a feeling . . . Darlis is everything I've been looking for since I was sixteen . . . and I'm really grateful to God that I found her . . . I'm in love, I'm in love—Wow!"

There was another surprise at the end, because I had written, ". . . he asked me Monday night and got the ring Tuesday (he chose it by himself and I love it) . . . we just feel made for each other and I couldn't be happier . . . I'm glad he feels so happy too."

Looking up from the letter I said, "Isn't it great that we still feel the same way?" He replied, "Yes, but can you imagine someone saving a letter forty-eight years? I'm so glad she sent this. We'll save it too."

There's an even older love letter that has been sent to each of us. The Bible is so full of words expressing God's love that it's hard to choose only a few, but Jeremiah 31:3 says, "I have loved you with an everlasting love . . ."

Do you think *I love you* should be proven with actions? God thought so. "This is how God showed His love among us: He sent His one and only Son into the world that we might live through Him. This is love; not that we loved God, but that He loved us and sent His Son as an atoning sacrifice for our sins" (1 John 4:9-10). God said, "I love you," and Jesus said, "I love you, too," as he humbled himself to come to earth as a baby—living, loving proof of God's love.

Some people think God's love letter is too long and too hard to read. Relax. The Bible is considered a collection of sixty-six books of various lengths. You don't have to read them all or understand every word to get the meaning of its message. Try reading about Jesus, God's love in action, in one of the *Good News* books labeled *Matthew, Mark, Luke* and *John*. You'll find a love letter that only God could write.

WHAT IS LOVE?
By Darlis Sailors

LOVE is fragile,
Like a flower in bloom.
Nurture it carefully,
Let it grow.

LOVE is challenging,
Like a trail in the woods.
Explore it slowly,
Discover its joy.

LOVE is valuable,
Worth effort and time.
Invest it thoughtfully,
Reap the rewards.

LOVE is emotional,
Up, down, twirled around.
Buckle your seatbelt,
Risk the ride.

LOVE is sharing,
Both laughter and tears
Open your heart,
Widen your world.

MOVING ON

I was married and gone from home when my mom asked if I thought they had been good parents. I thought back upon the financial sacrifices they had made to take family vacations and put food on the table. I also remembered help with school projects and their teaching of moral and spiritual values.

On the other hand, I thought of not being allowed to folk dance or square dance in gym, not being allowed to go to a friend's birthday party because they were going to a Disney movie, and not being allowed to read even a Christian book for teens about sex.

I shared some of the negatives with Mom, but told her overall I felt she and Dad had done a good job of raising us. Her question helped me realize I had felt like a victim under some of their restraints; however, instead of anger and rehearsing complaints against the way I was raised, I had moved on to my own choices. I was an adult now, out on my own. Life choices were mine, not theirs.

The first movie I ever attended was *Sound of Music,* and twenty-two years after that childhood birthday party I went to see *Bambi,* just to see what I had missed. I chose to read Christian books about sex and marriage, but I never learned to dance because I discovered I had two left feet.

The things I had to deal with were not life-threatening like some childhood issues people must overcome; however, they did affect my life view and who I was. Parenting skills do not arrive in a neat little package along with a baby's birth, so most parents struggle with "How will I do this?"

I believe we all grow up with some residual effects of our upbringing. As youngsters we are taught to respect our parents, teachers and elders. They have great influence upon our lives, but for how long?

Moving on from childhood to adulthood brings change. The Apostle Paul said, "When I was a child, I talked like a child, I thought like a child, I reasoned like a child. When I became a man, I put the ways of childhood behind me" (1 Corinthians 13:11). Maturity means growing in ability to take personal responsibility for our choices.

A physical move usually includes sorting things out and boxing them up to give away. Moving on into maturity may include some sorting out and letting go of emotional baggage from our childhood. The nice thing is, there's no age limit on that move.

THE BROKEN BULLDOG

When a friend was commenting on something she had done forty years ago, she said, "My mother seems to bring it up from time to time. I don't think she's ever forgiven me." That brought to mind "the bulldog incident" with *my* mom. Not that she ever brought it up over the years. She didn't need to, because I never forgot it.

I was in the third grade and my class had "Show and Tell." In a nine-month school year lots of things would have been shared, but the one thing I remember is mom's broken bulldog.

That small ceramic knick-knack, about two inches high and three inches long, was special to her and intriguing to me. I begged to take it for "Show and Tell," but she consistently refused. I would not give up. "I'll take good care of it," I promised for the umpteenth time. Finally, she relented and I proudly headed off to school clutching my prize in a small brown bag.

My school was a two-story, brick building and my classroom was on the second level. I couldn't believe what happened. I tripped UP the stairs! Naturally I was embarrassed, but I was horrified at the tinkling sound as my hand slammed down to gain my balance. When I got to the top of the stairs and looked in the bag, my heart fell. The little dog was in tiny pieces.

I remember the sad look on mom's face when I walked into the house after school, explained what happened and showed her the evidence. Her simple response was a quiet, resigned, "Oh, Darlis." She never reminded me of the incident, but I always wished for a replacement. I never found one, but years later I tried to give her a small ceramic dog of another species. She was not impressed.

I learned a couple of things from the bulldog incident. First, do not expect good results from willful, headstrong choices. King Saul learned the same lesson. He chose to make a sacrifice to God, instead of waiting for the prophet to do it. Samuel arrived late, according to Saul's time table, and his message from the Lord was, ". . . to obey is better than sacrifice . . ." (1 Samuel 15:22).

Second, I learned the truth of the old saying, "There is never a right way to do a wrong thing." Doing good works will never make up for disobedience. So, what's the solution? First John 1:9 (KJV) says, "If we confess our sins, he is faithful and just to forgive us our sins, and to cleanse us from all unrighteousness." No condemnation, no reminders, just a clean, fresh start. What could be better than that? To me, mom was an example of God's kind of forgiveness.

The broken bulldog taught me the value of obedience and it still remains a good reminder.

THE HONOR ROLE

A few years back, I had the privilege of talking with a young college graduate about some heartfelt issues. Her father, who had divorced and remarried, still lived in the area but did not keep in touch. Her mother had moved out of state but kept in close contact. This lovely Christian girl wanted to do the right thing by both parents.

The Bible says we are to honor our father and mother (Exodus 20:12; Deuteronomy 5:16; Matthew 15:4). Warm fuzzy feelings may or may not come with it, but we are assigned to play *The Honor Role*. What is it? How is it done?

Anyone desiring to honor another is starting from the right point, *humility*---a willingness to declare someone as more important than themselves. We did not get to choose our parents, but we do get to choose how we will treat them. As children we were to obey, but part of growing up is to be able to make decisions for ourselves. So, let's look at some *Honor Role* options:

RESPECT: Treating your parents with consideration and appreciation. For example, is a card or phone call too much to ask as acknowledgement of them on special days?

ESTEEM: Valuing the roles played out in their lives before you were born. After all, parents are people, too. They made choices based on things you may never know or understand.

ACCEPTANCE: Your parents may not have been what you wished for, and you may have even struggled to survive, but cutting them off, or out of your life, leaves a sore spot in all of you.

RECOGNITION: You have a role to play and no one can do it for you. A spouse or sibling trying to cover up by adding your name to a card or gift is not the same as you taking an interest and participating in that act of recognition

I'm happy to report that this young lady took her role seriously. She let her father know that she wanted a relationship with him, including his new wife and family. She had no guarantees, but she humbled herself, opened the door and waited for his response.

His response was positive. A few years later her father passed away suddenly, but because of her earlier decision to play *The Honor Role* she had no regrets.

Perhaps you have already fulfilled that role. If not, and your parents are still living, take advantage of the honoring options still open to you.

WATCH FOR ATMs

Automated Teller Machines (ATMs) are everywhere these days. Banks began this customer service and then it became so popular that people looked for it in other places. Busy consumers loved the convenience of withdrawals, deposits and access to balances without actually going into their bank.

I'd like to point out that ATMs have been around since the beginning of time. All cultures have enjoyed easy access to them. I'm talking about **A**lert **T**eachable **M**oments—those times when a child's interest is high and they simply want to know *why*. Or, maybe it's when they have made a mistake and don't want to do it again.

Family settings are filled with ATMs because they have first access to the child; however, their use is not limited to parents since friends, teachers and others have ATM options, too.

Everyone knows that family life can become hectic while trying to meet a variety of needs and schedules. It's easy for adults to whiz right by the ATM while also pushing the off switch on their child's inquisitive engine.

God is quite aware of the value of ATMs. In Deuteronomy 11:19 He said, "Teach (these words of mine) to your children, talking about them when you sit at home and when you walk along the road, when you lie down and when you get up." Today the house might be a condo or apartment and the road might be a sidewalk or paved street. Lying down could be bedtime or naptime and getting up would be the way you start your day in any culture.

I have happy ATM memories of a curious preschooler. We used to walk her neighborhood and those short walks were filled with teachable moments. Such special moments are fleeting. Like blown bubbles they are there, then gone.

Children basically arrive ready and open to learning about their world; however, teachable moments are not always wordy. Children are observant and sometimes the example you set will do.

Teachable moments can result in cute stories and good humor since children don't understand words on the adult level. You might have recognized an ATM and deposited into it quite wisely, but when you asked for the receipt, or feedback, you were surprised by the misconception.

Based upon my years of ministry experience, I'm convinced human ATMs are not limited to children. Since these opportunities stem from relationships, teens and adults of all ages benefit from them, too. These **A**lert **T**eachable **M**oments, though brief, are powerful. Be aware. Use them whenever and wherever you can.

CHAPTER TWO

FOOD FACTORS

A BASKET OF LEMONS

One day when I was looking at a basket of colorful pink grapefruit and bright yellow lemons, I was reminded how easy it is to say, "When life gives you lemons, make lemonade." In reality, it's a rather messy time-consuming process but we enjoy the sweetness when it's finished.

I recently heard a Scripture read that sounded like a basketful of lemons. It listed six problems with two common denominators, *cause of stress* and *need for a timely solution.* The lemons included non-budding fig trees, fruitless grapevines, olive crop failure, fields yielding no food, plus empty sheep pens and cattle stalls (Habakkuk 3:17).

Current examples might include lack of finances, broken or strained relationships, jobs or no job, health challenges, and losses of various kinds.

Which of the above lemons could be turned into lemonade overnight? Life is full of challenges or tests that require time to overcome, and that requires perseverance, best described with the famous quote by Winston Churchill: "Never, never, never give up."

Perseverance includes maintaining faith in God and rejoicing as He enables us to move up and out of our hard places as if we were fleet-footed deer (Habakkuk 3:18-19). In the mountains where we live, I have watched in amazement as deer have come to a steep bank, leaped up and moved out of sight. I have also seen them leap fences and continue down a bank so steep that cars traverse it with hairpin curves. These deer are awesome. Perseverance in action!

I originally wrote the following poem to encourage a friend to persevere, but later I found I needed it myself. Now I keep it handy to share with others.

ONWARD TO VICTORY
By Darlis Sailors

Life is bitter, where once it was sweet.
Faith feels worthless, and prayers seem weak.

But faith is not feelings, so onward you go
Into battle with power to meet every foe.

God's Word gives you hope; His presence empowers.
There's victory ahead, just not at this hour.

The timing is His, but joy will be sweet
When testing is over—your victory complete.

A TOXIC ROOT

My mother and I, though both ministers' wives, were opposite in the way we approached the Bible. I enjoy regular use of Bible study workbooks. She preferred to read the Bible through in a different version every year. We were alike, however, in our desire to live out what we studied or read.

One time when I was visiting, she was in her favorite rocker/recliner reading the Bible as usual. As I walked past I casually asked, "Mom, what is your favorite verse?" She said, "Great peace have they which love thy law; and nothing shall offend them" (Psalm 119:165, KJV).

I was so surprised that I stopped and said, "Why would that be important to you now, Mom? You haven't been working with a congregation for several years." I knew from experience that people working with people offered opportunities to be offended, simply because none of us are perfect.

She just said, "It's very important to me," and that was all. As I have thought back over it these past years, I respect her answer more than ever. I can see by my response that I was not ready to really understand. Besides, she had a right to keep her personal reasons personal.

I have done a lot of study on Hebrews 12:14-15 and verse fifteen backs up the one Mom quoted: "See to it that . . . no bitter root grows up to cause trouble and defile many." Like a taproot, an offense can remain hidden, yet affect everything which can be seen above it.

Pull up a baby carrot with a dangling thread-like root and you think *that's nothing*. But left to grow for a longer time the root becomes stronger and you have to pull harder to loosen the soil and pull the veggie out. Even then you won't enjoy the aroma of fresh carrot until the dirt is washed off.

That's why the advice in Hebrews is important. Catch that root of bitterness in the thread-like stage. Don't let it become a strong taproot. Offended people can come across as annoyed or angry, outraged, insulted or resentful. Instead of sweetness in their approach to others, there is acidity which eats away at relationships.

We are planted in this garden of life together and we each have roots which need our personal attention. The verse I referred to in Hebrews 12:14 says a root of bitterness will cause trouble and *defile* others as it grows. To *defile* something is to pollute, corrupt or contaminate it. That's not the way I want to affect people, do you?

Holding on to an offense shows that we are focused more on ourselves than we are on God. Self-absorption is fertile soil for a toxic root, but the remedy is in mom's verse. If you love God's Word above yourself, great peace is possible. I'd rather have that, wouldn't you?

ACCIDENTAL SPAGHETTI SAUCE

I took a small package of ground beef out of my freezer. I planned to make *Porcupine Meatballs*, a childhood favorite. I had made them before, so I didn't pull a recipe.

The next day I put the hamburger in a large bowl, along with rice and seasoning. I carefully washed my hands and mixed up the meatballs, my least favorite part.

I had already put the tomato sauce into the crock pot, so I dropped in the small hand-shaped balls, making sure all were completely covered. I looked at the time and decided an hour on high, then on low while I was gone for the afternoon should be fine.

Dinner time! The meatballs smelled so good and I was hungry. In great anticipation I turned off the crock pot and removed the lid. The sauce was bubbling hot so I let it cool a little before I anxiously used a fork to pull out a sample meatball.

Oh, no! It fell apart. It didn't do that before. Where did I go wrong? I got out a recipe. There it was---one simple mistake. I had left out the egg. No wonder it didn't hold together. I knew I wouldn't make that mistake again, but what should I do with this mushy meatball mess? It didn't appeal to me as soup.

After it was totally cool, I separated it into two parts, one for the freezer, the other for the refrigerator. I'd have to wait for an idea on how to use it.

A couple of days later it hit me. Why not try it in spaghetti sauce? My husband loves meat in his pasta and I had commercial sauce on hand. I put my refrigerated mistake into a small pan on the stove and covered it with plenty of red sauce.

As I served my husband spaghetti with meaty sauce, he was singing my praises. I confessed. "This was really a mistake." He said, "You didn't make this great sauce on purpose?" I said, "No, it's accidental spaghetti sauce. I skipped the recipe and forgot the egg so there were no meatballs, just mush."

I thought *this illustrates how God works all things together for our good.* I was so disappointed when I realized I had messed up, but I waited for an idea to help me redeem the mess I had made. When a solution came, it was good.

As humans we make mistakes quite often, some more life-changing than others. But if we wait upon God, who sees all things for what they truly are, He comes up with a way to work what we consider a mess-up into something good for us and also for His glory and purpose for us. Surprisingly, our mess can even bless. "ALL things are possible with God" (Mark 10:27).

CARROT CAKE LADY

Once upon a time in the great southwest, I met a lady who grew up on the coast of New Jersey. She attended a Bible college in the Midwest and fell in love with a young man who felt called to be a preacher. They married and were blessed with two sons whom they enjoyed raising in the small towns where they ministered.

This lady enjoyed cooking and baking. Hospitality was definitely one of her gifts. She enjoyed being a mom and a preacher's wife, but when necessary she made time to work outside the home. She was a petite dark-haired woman with an engaging smile and a dry sense of humor. She had a calm demeanor and it was easy to relax in her home.

My husband and I were recipients of her hospitality and delicious home-cooked meals many times, but our special memories always include her carrot cake. You can't forget a yummy cake like that . . . made from scratch and covered with rich cream cheese frosting. She would bake it in an oblong pan, turn it out on a foil-covered cardboard and frost it as beautifully as if it came from a bakery. We would share it as dessert after the meal and she would send the rest of it home with us. I would freeze it in two-piece sections to make it last as long as possible.

But there was another special thing about those carrot cakes. Not only were they homemade, they were birthday gifts! This busy pastor's wife believed birthdays were important and her way of making people feel special was with her time-consuming, energy-requiring homemade carrot cake.

In my home, birthdays had not been very special occasions. I was awed by this lady's special consideration of them, not only for us but for so many others.

Year after year she remembered the birthday of an older man in a care center. One time she asked, "How old are you today?" He said, "I'm ninety." She laughed and said, "You're ninety-one. I'm keeping track."

This lovely Christian lady lived out a verse in Galatians 6:10 which says, "As we have opportunity, let us do good to all people, especially to those who belong to the family of believers." Based on her example, I've asked myself, "What good do I do when I have opportunity? Is it something planned, like her carrot cakes? Or, is it an opportunity that pops us where I do good spontaneously?" For me, spontaneity wins out. How about you?

MORE EGGS AND TOMATOES

As a child I used to think being kind was not fighting with my brothers, not being selfish with my toys or not grabbing the last cookie on the plate. I grew up with the King James Version of Ephesians 4:32 (KJV) which said, "Be ye kind one to another." That portion of the verse was simple enough for a young child to memorize and apply to life, but as an adult it meant much more.

By then I had learned that being kind meant more than not being selfish. To be kind meant to be concerned about others, not as one big *do-all* but in *little seeds of kindness* every day.

These positive seeds/deeds can be scattered about, unnoticed by anyone but those who need them. Things like an encouraging word to the weary, a cup of coffee and a listening ear---even when there are no answers to give, a card that says *Thinking of You,* or something done to meet a specific need that won't let go of your heart.

Kindness can turn up in an act so small that you don't even remember doing it. Some people call it "doing a good turn."

In our early-married years, we began full-time ministry in a small church with a growing congregation. My husband was their first associate pastor and the salary was small, but we were grateful to also be given housing nearby.

The budget was tight, but as a newly-wed I enjoyed reading grocery ads and planning low-cost meals. Utilities were high and we did not need all three bedrooms, so we shut off two of them to make it easier for the wall heater in the living area to heat the house. Living next door to the church eased car expenses, but parishioner kindness had an impact on our lives, too.

One of the founding families started bringing us home-grown tomatoes and a flat of eggs quite regularly. We received them joyfully. One time as I was thanking them, the husband said, "We drive to an egg ranch up in the hills and it's just as easy to buy two flats as one." They continued their weekly blessings until we were able to purchase a home and move out of the parsonage.

We later left that ministry and moved to another state, but returned about ten years later after we received a call offering further ministry options. The church had really grown but it was nice to see the family that had been so kind to us in our early years.

One time, as we tried to tell them how their constant supply of eggs and tomatoes had blessed us, we were astounded when they said they did not remember doing that!

If you respond to an opportunity to do good, there is no reason it should stick in your mind. But it may remain forever in the mind of the one who experiences it. We have never forgotten those eggs and tomatoes. In fact, those *seeds of kindness* have born much fruit over the years because we have tried to repay them by *paying it forward.*

MORE FRUIT, PLEASE

I can't imagine life without fruit. It would be much less satisfying because I enjoy the taste of apple in a Waldorf salad and sweet strawberries in a nice cool smoothie. Of course, bananas can be used in lots of ways, but three scoops of ice cream with different toppings just seem more fun served as a Banana Split.

Fruit satisfies and meets needs even when it stands alone. Who hasn't heard the old adage "an apple a day keeps the doctor away"? Fresh strawberries or a nice ripe peach are very satisfying, but don't ignore a green banana. With a little more time it will become a sweet treat.

At the market I always look for strawberries and grapes from California because I lived where they are grown, but I enjoy fruit from places I have never seen. My presence is not required for them to grow. I simply enjoy the results of someone else's labor. We know that fruit is important for our nutritional health, but Scriptures teach about fruit that is important to our spiritual lives.

We find this spiritual fruit has different qualities, as explained in Galatians 5:13-26. Fruit produced by a sinful nature requires laws to keep it under control. On the other hand, the fruit of God's Spirit has no laws against it. There are nine character traits, or *fruit of the Sprit*, listed in Galatians 5:22-23. Produced in the lives of believers anywhere in the world, they would have the same result. *Givers* would be delighted to have such good fruit to share and *receivers* would find the fruit tasteful and satisfying.

As a child I memorized the names of the fruit of the Spirit from what is now the New King James Version of the Bible. But I like the explanation of each one in The Message Bible.

For example, LOVE is explained as *affection for others.* JOY is *exuberance about life.* PEACE is *serenity.* LONGSUFFERING is a *willingness to stick with things.* KINDNESS is *a sense of compassion in the heart.* GOODNESS is *conviction that a basic holiness permeates things and people.* FAITHFULNESS is *being involved in loyal commitments.* GENTLENESS is *not needing to force our way in life,* and SELF-CONTROL means being *able to marshal and direct our energies wisely.*

It was nice to earn points in Sunday School for quickly naming the nine character qualities produced by the Holy Spirit. But their real value was gained as I allowed them to mature in my life and how I shared them while relating to others.

An old song says, "They will know we are Christians by our love," but why be satisfied with one fruit out of nine? When in prayer, don't be afraid to ask for, "More Fruit, Please."

ONE CARELESS BAKER

I enjoy old-fashioned recipes where individual ingredients are to be measured and added together, one at a time. I have a recipe for cornbread that I have made for years and I wouldn't say I have it memorized, but I don't spend much time looking at the recipe.

Recently I found an easy ready-made cornbread mix that required only the addition of water. One morning I made my way to the kitchen and set the oven to my usual cornbread temperature before prepping the mix and pouring it into the baking pan. As I opened the oven I noticed a red glow. I paused a minute. *I don't think I've noticed that red before. It must be part of the preheating process.* I set the pan inside, closed the door and set the timer per package instructions.

Instead of waiting for the timer to go off, I checked the cornbread at my old recipe's recommended twenty minutes. It had a toasty brown top and when I slipped in a knife, it came out clean. Done!

Thinking *it's a good thing I checked, because ten more minutes would have been a disaster*, I left the cornbread on a rack to cool and went ahead with another baking project. When it was ready, I reached to set the oven on a new temperature. That's when I noticed the oven setting had been on broil. No wonder there was a red glow!

I scolded myself for being so careless and glanced over at the cornbread only to be horrified by a deep sinkhole in its middle. I tried re-baking that cornbread at lower temperatures for short periods of time but I never did fully redeem it. The edges were fine, but the center always remained a little mushy.

I'm thinking that sometimes we become like careless bakers in our Christian living. We may have been believers for a long time and think we know Christian basics of faith, hope and love quite well. Instead of getting out our Bibles to bone up on instructions, we tell ourselves, "There's no need to review. I've done this for so long that I know what I'm doing."

There's an important list of spiritual character ingredients we don't want to miss in 2 Peter 1:3-11. The New King James Version says they are to be *added to each other*. Just as my cornbread mix grew as I added ingredients, our spiritual life grows gradually, too.

The first spiritual ingredient is *faith.* To that we add *virtue*, or goodness. To virtue we add *knowledge* and to knowledge, *self-control,* followed by *perseverance*. Next on the list is *godliness*, enhanced by *brotherly kindness* and capped off by *love*.

Avoid being a careless spiritual baker. Take time to open your Bible, read for vital directions and follow them. Don't take things for granted, like I did with the cornbread. If you stay alert, you'll enjoy satisfying results.

THE TIMING OF AN EGG

Some wise person said, "Don't count your chickens before they're hatched." If you grew up on a farm, you probably know the value of that advice. But if you were a city girl like me, you probably consider it a nice cliché. As a child, eggs were not my favorite until it was time to dye them for Easter baskets. That meant that after Easter I had to eat eggs in a variety of ways, but I accepted that as a reasonable trade-off for the fun of decorating them each year.

A grade school friend often invited me to share her country life, and I still have a warm spot in my heart for life on the farm. One of her chores was collecting eggs, which I thought was fun to watch. In reality, I wasn't much help with my skittish behavior around the hens, but she just laughed and calmly completed her chore.

Fertilized eggs are capable of producing chickens if incubated for the proper amount of time at the required temperature. Getting anxious and disturbing the eggs to see if anything has happened yet might cause disappointment twice, once when eggs are checked prematurely and later, when they fail to hatch.

You may have heard of *brooding hens*, waiting for their eggs to produce little chickens. Humans brood, too, but we refer to it as being moody, anxious, or worried when something is taking longer than expected.

Goals, for example, need time to hatch. Have you ever set a goal and started working toward it only to keep thinking *nothing is developing, so why am I wasting my time?* Because you can't see the expected result in your time frame, you are tempted to think your goal no longer has value.

Things like educational or career goals may be hatching out nicely, but slower to develop is a relationship of importance to you. You have tried to allow time for it to hatch, but it seems lifeless. Since there is no time chart for the development of human relationships, you brood over it wondering *what should I do?*

I brooded over a medical diagnosis and long-term treatment plan. As friends and family prayed for me, they would ask, "How are you doing?" I had the same question as I turned over the eggs of medical reports, doctor's comments and hope for my progress, only to find that my expectations were premature. Giving up was not an option, so I decided to hatch good health by following the advice in Psalm 27:14 which says, "Wait for the Lord; be strong and take heart and wait for the Lord." "Wait" was the word of the day.

Not counting your chickens before they are hatched is good advice, but eggs, in general, need to be handled with care. The timing of an egg, no matter what kind you're working with, includes waiting. Given time, you may find the results were worth the wait.

CHAPTER THREE

INTERNAL AFFAIRS

A VERY BAD HAIR DAY

It used to be so easy to get frustrated with bad haircuts and flat-hair days. My hair is fine and I had perms for years, until one time a stylist refused to give me the perm that was on sale. That was all my budget could afford, so I settled for a short cut and started living with straight hair.

At various times I still lived with curlers and hair dryers, back-combing and hair spray. Like most women, I complained about "a bad hair day" while getting ready to go somewhere. But in 2007 I experienced the worst bad hair day ever! I brushed my hair and it fell into the sink. I stared down at the clumps of hair, then picked up a hand mirror to survey the damage.

As I faced the bathroom mirror there was no sparkle in my eyes, no bright smile, just an incredible amount of sadness. I'd had two chemo treatments, been warned of side effects, and now my day of reckoning had come. I asked my husband to cut off the remaining patches of hair. Why put off the inevitable?

I was prepared with a wig, but the feel of it on my bald head was not comfortable. Another problem was a cold head at night, since I slept under air conditioning as respite from the desert heat.

I tried to find a knit cap for bedtime, but the summer sales associates in each store just shook their heads at my inquiry. I rarely wore my wig because I was much more comfortable in a square cotton scarf, knotted behind my neck.

I found timely comfort in 1 Peter 3:3-4. It says beauty is not to come from *outward adornment*, but from *your inner self.*

This inner beauty is described as *unfading*, and includes *a gentle and quiet spirit* which God considers of great value.

Solomon was quite blunt when comparing beauty basics both inward and outward. He said, "Like a gold ring in a pig's snout is a beautiful woman who shows no discretion" (Proverbs 11:22). Discretion is not automatic; it requires applying some self-control. The good news was that I could pursue inner beauty in spite of my bald head.

In the reality of life, it's not only women who have *bad-hair days*. I have yet to meet a man who actually enjoys growing bald. Some choose to shave their head completely to get it over with, much like I did when I asked my husband for help.

The inner quality of self-control is as important to men as it is to women. Solomon shared a manly illustration when he said, "Like a city whose walls are broken down is the man who lacks self-control" (Proverbs 25:28). A broken down city is not a pretty sight and can even be dangerous.

I'm very thankful to have hair now, and I try not to lose my focus on bad-hair days. Beauty from the inside out was a lesson learned and if I remember to apply that secret ingredient of self-control, it still works wonders.

CALIFORNIA GOLD

Who wouldn't enjoy having more gold as a personal budget booster? I used to get a kick out of hearing The Oakridge Boys sing about all the gold in California being "in the middle of a bank in Beverly Hills under somebody else's name."

I didn't think much about it until I served Rick some appetizing orange slices on his breakfast plate, long after we had left that state.

"M-m-m, delicious," he said, "where did you get these?"

"Walmart. Seventy cents each."

"What! Each?"

"That's right. Kind of hard for a boy raised in Central California to understand, isn't it?"

"Yes, it is. Dad must have had hundreds of dollars hanging on those four orange trees out by the old garage."

We used to bring them into the house by the bucketful. But I took those big juicy oranges for granted, along with other free items I had to purchase when we moved from that area. Things like strawberries, grapes, asparagus, kiwi, peaches, lemons, grapefruit and persimmons seemed priced like gold!

The Bible lists nine, invaluable character qualities called The Fruit of the Spirit. Absolutely no price can be put on those (Galatians 5:22-23), but did you know the Bible says your faith is more precious than gold? That's quite a comparison since gold is a commodity in great demand. I see a lot of signs around town that say, "We Buy Gold," but they don't want nuggets straight from the mine. They want pure gold.

Gold of that quality comes from a refiner's fire. Heat removes impurities. Life is full of hard spots, rough patches, troubles, trials or whatever you want to call them, but our faith, tested by fire and proved genuine, brings glory to God (1 Peter 1:7). God is interested in gold, but it's not the gold in California. It's what is in our hearts.

CORE CONCEPT

I always love it when my husband brings me flowers. I have a variety of vases on hand because I enjoy cutting stems and arranging flowers to show off their colors and shapes.

The first thing I do, after cutting open the cellophane wrapper, is to look for the packet of preservative. I pour it in the vase and add water. These tiny crystals allow me to enjoy my flowers up to nearly two weeks, if I add water now and then and keep them out of direct sunlight.

Sometimes the bouquets are natural flowers and greenery, but once in a while he brings daisies or carnations which have been artificially colored. I love color, so I don't care which way it comes, natural or man-made.

Recently he brought a beautiful bouquet of yellow, lavender and fuchsia daisies. I got out a tall vase and snipped away, plunging the stems into the clear, treated water. Satisfied with the color arrangement, I tied a gold ribbon around the neck of the vase and set it in the living area to enjoy.

Most of the flowers still looked good a week later, but the water was pink-toned. I took the vase to the kitchen, pulled out the flowers and poured the water into a smaller vase. A few of the flowers had wilted, but I shortened the stems on the flowers which still had life. Now I had a smaller, but still colorful, arrangement.

The next morning, my husband noticed the flowers on our kitchen table and asked, "Why is the water pink?" I said, "The pink and purple daisies were artificially colored. Florists put dye into the water and the flowers absorb it up through their stem and out into the petals. Now the color is seeping out, so we see pinkish-purple water."

As I stared at that vase I thought *we're no different from the flowers. What we take in, we give out.* It's hard to give out positive thoughts if we have filled our mind with negative ones. A spirit of cooperation will never seep out of a person who has not soaked up the skills needed to be a team player. Love becomes discolored in a heart full of jealousy, and generosity will not come flowing out of a heart saturated in selfishness.

The human core concept is explained well in Luke 6:45 where we read, "A good man brings good things out of the good stored up in his heart, and an evil man brings evil things out of the evil stored up in his heart. For the mouth speaks what the heart is full of." When I was in the office world that concept was applied to computers as *garbage in---garbage out.*

It's been said that "You can fool some of the people some of the time, but you can't fool all of the people all of the time." What's in our core will eventually seep out. There's no hiding forever, not even from ourselves, what's in our heart.

DEAR WILL

If this was titled "Dear John," you would expect it to be a story about letting someone go. A "Dear John" letter is probably as hard to send as it is to receive since broken relationships are synonymous with sorrow, tears and regret.

My "Dear Will" letter is written to celebrate a positive aspect of our personalities, the ability to choose. It makes us human and determines our quality of life. Even in the hardest of circumstances we can decide how to respond. That's worth celebrating!

Dear Will,

What a pleasure to write this letter. I want you to know how much I appreciate having you in my life.

Thanks to you, I can make thoughtful decisions and not rush blindly into dangerous situations. You are the one who enables me to choose what to do, where to go, and what to say. I appreciate the freedom you give me and how you wait while I search things out and review information to make a good choice.

Because of you I am captain of my own ship in many ways. Even when the storms of life cause me grief and troubled times, I don't have to bob along on unsettled waves. I can decide which life-saving actions to pursue.

I have learned from experience that you can be quite flexible. If I need strength and boldness, you rise to the occasion and people call me "strong-willed." If I choose to shrink back and let circumstances and others' choices control me, I get labeled "weak-willed." Either way, you stick with me.

I appreciate your respect. Others may try to pressure me into doing their will by threatening to affect my life in any number of uncomfortable ways, but you quietly wait in the background for my decision. Once it's made, you support me while I follow through.

I thank God for you, Will. You have helped make me who I am today and will continue to impact my life right to the end. You accompany me as a companion, not a dictator. My wrong choices cause discomfort, but you remain loyal, hoping I will see the error of my ways. I consider you an invaluable friend.

Marriage ceremonies include Ruth's famous use of *Will* when she decided to move with her mother-in-law to a foreign country. She firmly stated, "Where you go I will go, and where you stay I will stay . . . where you die I will die, and there will I be buried" (Ruth 1:16-17).

Prior to the crucifixion, *Will* appeared when Jesus prayed to his Father, "Take this cup from me. Yet not what I will, but what you will" (Mark 14:36).

Will helps shape my life and I'm grateful. How about you?

FROGS WITH PERSONALITY

What fascinates me about people is our differences. I don't mean our physical characteristics, since worldwide we each have body parts in common. What makes each of us unique is our personality, or what some call our *temperament*.

I have had the privilege of hearing Florence Littauer speak and I have read her books about personality traits. She mentions four basic groups: *Sanguine* (let's have fun); *Choleric* (I want control); *Melancholy* (I desire perfection); and *Phlegmatic* (let's keep it peaceful). Of course, it's not that simple but it's a start. Her books explain these four in more detail, and combinations seem endless as traits from one type can be combined with those in another. A few years ago, I took her Personality Profile test and my results were *Melancholy/Phlegmatic*.

Shortly after that, I went to apply for a job and was surprised to hear my potential manager ask if I knew my personality type. I said, "It's Melancholy/Phlegmatic." She sparked right up and said, "That's what I'm looking for!" I got the job and we made a great team.

I came to appreciate these two traits. My *Melancholy* side paid attention to necessary details, while my *Phlegmatic* side helped me be a team player. But what do frogs have to do with this?

One night, after watching *Cheaper by the Dozen* on DVD, my husband and I took time for the behind-the-scenes features. The animal trainer caught my attention as he talked about the family dinner scene where everyone is trying to catch a frog that is jumping around, causing pandemonium.

I was surprised to hear the trainer say, "We had two types of frogs, sitters and jumpers. Not all frogs like to jump, so we had some of each to be prepared for the director's needs." He made his living by knowing the sitters from the jumpers, so I'll take his word for it.

Humans are more complicated. When you think of all the people you know, isn't it amazing that four basic categories can be entwined to create an endless variety of temperaments?

Whenever I read Psalm 139, I praise God for the marvels of our physical bodies. But while learning about personality traits, I saw many more reasons to praise God for His creative wisdom.

Our personalities are as different as our fingerprints, yet there are enough similarities to create reference charts such as those shared by Florence. Proverbs 3:13 declares there is a blessing in gaining understanding.

I really enjoyed learning about personality traits because it helped me understand myself, as well as others. I'll admit our human personalities can get a bit complicated, but I'm so glad that God didn't just create us as sitters or jumpers.

FROM HEART TO HANDS

We have a large and lovely decorator clock in our living area. The rim is dark and the face is white with gold trim. Decorative figures adorn the inner edges and a sparkly piece twirls continually inside the oval base.

As much as we enjoy the outer features, the unseen inner workings are the important thing. Thanks to the movements in the heart, the hands go around and we are treated to a short melody from a popular love song, once every hour. We find it very satisfying since the clock was a fortieth anniversary gift from longtime friends on our celebration weekend. There was joy as they gave it and joy as we received it.

The inner workings of our spiritual heart move our hands to do things, too. James said, "I will show you my faith by my deeds" (James 2:18). Faith is a good thing, since it's the starting point of coming to God, believing that He exists and rewards those who earnestly seek Him (Hebrews 11:6). But James didn't want believers just to be like the decorative part of a wall clock. He wanted inner workings of faith to produce some good deeds, something that would meet needs and bring people joy.

In James 2:14-18 he shared a practical illustration by saying, "Suppose a brother or a sister is without clothes and daily food. If one of you says to them, 'Go in peace; keep warm and well fed,' but does nothing about their physical needs, what good is it?" Activate your faith. Do something.

My husband and I activate our heartfelt faith in different ways. For example, he is well-blessed with coats and sweaters, so he has carried extras in his car during cold weather and offered them to people in need of something warmer.

I, on the other hand, seem aware of people in need of food. Sometimes I share items person-to-person from our pantry or freezer and other times I buy specific items. Food bank flyers and food drives always catch my attention.

In December, people's hearts seem more motivated to give. Hands generously drop dollars into red kettles, collect items for food banks, buy gifts to meet needs on Angel Trees and donate toys and other items to charitable organizations

Donations are very important and bless many, but charitable institutions and ministries meet needs all year long. That's why, like the inner workings of a clock, our heartfelt giving should not simply be seasonal.

We enjoy hourly tunes from our musical clock on a daily basis. Maybe we do not produce good deeds so regularly, but there's no need to wait for December. We can be motivated from heart to hands to meet needs and show our faith all year long.

SANDY SECRETS

I had the unexpected pleasure of going to Egypt without flying over the ocean or needing a passport. The Arizona Science Center in Phoenix had a short-term exhibit called LOST EGYPT: Ancient Secrets, Modern Science.

Up on the third floor, I began with a display about the desert pyramids. Huge photos showed that rough-hewn blocks created the basic size and shape. Outer stones were then smoothed and hand shaped to fill in and create that perfect look we see in photos. It was easy to see why it took an average of twenty years to build one of these wonders.

I enjoyed hearing a young archeologist explain her space-age research. In a short video, she shared that in two weeks she can photographically search a one-thousand square-mile area from space. A ground team searching for archeological sites on that much land could take up to three-and-a-half years.

Meanwhile, an Egyptian archeologist, in a video on the other side of the room, explained that ground teams are still necessary. They visually search an area of interest by driving and walking. Moving from the simple to the complex they use tools to photograph, measure distance and height and create maps which will be useful to future archeological digs.

The next area had mummy displays of humans and animals. Modern science no longer requires specimens to be unwrapped slowly, layer by layer, while making careful notes and diagrams. Today much more detailed information is acquired by using x-rays, CT scans and other machines that doctors use to see inside our bodies. That means the mummy remains fully preserved, including the colorful face mask and artfully decorated overlays from head to toe.

I was surprised to learn how fragments of pottery reveal many secrets. Scientists look for clues in the type of clay, size, shape, style of decorating, or even the lack of it. I was amazed to read that by following such clues they could even determine trade routes, since I had just been reading about trade in King Solomon's time (1Kings 10). Now I could picture how pottery helped store and transport certain commodities.

The museum had other floors with modern secrets, but we had spent our time on ancient ones. I came away thinking of Jesus' words in Matthew 10:26. He said, "For there is nothing concealed that will not be disclosed or hidden that will not be made known." Deuteronomy 29:29 says, "The secret things belong to the Lord our God, but the things revealed belong to us and our children forever." I enjoyed Egypt's sandy secrets. They will not be forgotten.

STILL WATERS

Dad and I used to joke around with an old cliché. I'd say, "Still waters run deep." He'd laugh and say, "And cold, too." We had some great discussions about spirituality and I'm thankful for that heritage.

My teenage version of still waters was taking time to read my Bible nightly and meditating on verses before going to sleep. Bedtime was my choice because I was a night owl, not an early bird.

Life has a way of changing us, however. Now I get up, make breakfast and get my husband off to work in the early morning. Then I go to my office for time to relax with Scriptures for the day.

I enjoy Bible study workbooks and when a section or verse of Scripture stands out to me, I stop to mediate on it. I feel like a fisherman who has walked a trail down the riverbank, looking for a deep pool of still water. That's where the big fish might be found.

There have been times when I wandered away from the still waters and got lost temporarily in the bubbling, shallow waters of rocky times. But as I stayed near the river, I found my way back to spiritually refreshing times in quieter places.

We were privileged to see Niagara Falls close up, underneath those rushing waters. The noise was deafening, and everything was so wet and slick that we had to constantly be aware of where we were walking. It was a great experience, but what a relief to get up and away from the noise and pressure.

It's different with quiet waters. I want to return to a small pond or pool time after time, because still waters allow me to relax and contemplate the view. In fact, there is one small dry creek bed in the heart of our town that I always check out after the rains.

The cottonwood trees and wild grasses grow there all year long, but after a big rain I stop to enjoy the reflection of blue sky and white clouds in the still water. I may be looking down, but through reflection I'm also looking up. That's the way it is when I take time to read my Bible and meditate on it.

The Twenty-Third Psalm is probably the most famous of all of David's writings. It begins with "The Lord is my shepherd." It continues with assurance that He will provide what we need as He leads us in paths of righteousness for His name's sake.

He may lead, but will we follow? We all know water is basic to our health. You've heard it said about horses, and now I'll say it about sheep: "You can lead a sheep to water but you can't make it drink." How spiritually thirsty are you? Still waters, refreshing, reviving and accessible await you.

THE CHOICE IS OURS

Don't you enjoy shopping where a business keeps its word? Yesterday I stopped by a favorite coffee place to order my usual green tea with no sweetener and light ice.

They were extremely busy and the server was working quickly to keep up with orders. I waited patiently, along with those in line before and after me.

When my beverage was ready she called my name, set my drink on the counter and never looked up. As she went to work quickly on the next order, I picked up my tea and found it half full of ice.

I don't generally complain, but that was NOT what I had ordered. Then I noticed their sign. It said if I was not happy with my beverage I should let them know and they would make me another.

When she placed the next order on the counter I said, "Excuse me. This drink is half ice. I rarely drink ice at all, but I'll take a little bit." She asked me to remove the lid, dumped the tea down the sink and made a new one. Besides that, she looked me in the eye this time and gave me a smile. I walked out a happy customer because their sign meant what it said.

Spoken words are important, too. How many times have you shopped somewhere because someone told you there were bargains to be found? Or, maybe they said, "You can count on that company to keep their word." Positive personal recommendations always carry a lot of weight with me, since people freely share non-positive experiences, too. But the decision is always mine. Believe what I hear and act on it, or ignore it.

Jesus told a great story of two builders who each wanted a beach home. One built on the sand so he could enjoy the view and walk only a few steps to the water. The other man built away from the beach, up on some rocks. He also enjoyed a view but had to walk a little farther to go swimming.

A big storm came up and the house on the sand got wiped out. The one on the rocks never budged. Jesus said the builder on the rocks was wise, while the one on the sand was foolish. I picture Jesus, The Rock of our Salvation, placing a sign on the beach that says, "Build on the Rock . . . Free House Plans Available."

What He actually said was, "Everyone who hears these words of mine and puts them into practice is like a wise man who built his house on the rock" (Matthew 7:24-27).

Jesus' teachings are a solid foundation for life. It takes more effort to build on the rock than sand, but the choice is ours. Will we be wise or foolish?

WHATEVER!

When said with a shrug, "whatever" means a subject or decision has just been dismissed. No more thought will be given to it. Doris Day made the phrase *whatever will be, will be* famous, but it sounded so much catchier when sung as *Que Sera, Sera.*

I grew up with the King James Version of Philippians 4:8 which uses the word *whatsoever* six times. Here it is: *Finally, brethren, whatsoever things are true, whatsoever things are honest, whatsoever things are just, whatsoever things are pure, whatsoever things are lovely, whatsoever things are of good report; if there be any virtue, and if there be any praise, think on these things.*

Modern translations have changed *whatsoever* to *whatever*. Regardless of which word is used, the practicality of that verse is what has always intrigued me. Our minds wander easily from thought to thought, but they can be controlled.

I was fortunate to know a lady who lived to be ninety-four, and even in her declining years she determined to take charge of her mind. She was the mother of my best friend from college and I knew her for forty-eight years. Though her life was not easy, she had a sense of humor, practiced kindness and patience, read her Bible, and could be counted on to pray for people. She told her daughter, "I refuse to be a grumpy old lady."

As she entered her nineties, she worked daily to memorize Philippians 4:8 and quoted it to herself frequently. You can see how there is no room for negativity in such a focused mind.

When this lady passed away, her memorial service was packed with people who had been touched by her life. It was a pleasure to know her. She set a great example, but there's an old saying that "you have to do your own growing, no matter how tall your grandpa was." In this case it would be grandma, but she would say, "Each 'whatever' is by choice, not chance."

In thinking about our marvelous brain power, I wrote this poem. I hope it encourages you to activate your mind and take charge of your thoughts.

BRAINY MACHINE
By Darlis Sailors

There's a silent machine going 'round in my head,
Like cogs on a wheel in a wheel,
Or a curious cat darting this way and that,
Inspecting whatever appeals.

This little machine is powered by senses,
Five keep it turning quite well.
It prefers action to calm meditation,
But I can take charge at will.

Without thoughts in a jumble, just purpose and focus,
Its power comes under control
What a marvelous thing, this brainy machine,
I use it and life becomes whole.

CHAPTER FOUR

LIVING CONNECTED

A CHOICE of PATTERNS

When I think patterns, I think of my high school days and Home Economics. I enjoyed cooking and baking with patterns called recipes, but sewing was an entirely different matter. To this day I'm convinced the teacher could hardly wait for the semester to be over so I could permanently exit her class. I'll tell you why.

I was looking forward to learning to sew. I picked out a pattern, enjoyed shopping for materials and did a good job of pinning the pattern in place. Cutting around it didn't seem too hard. I wish I could say the same for those tiny "tacks."

By hand, I was to sew a loop through two pieces of material, then lift the top layer and snip through the loop. Each piece would then have little threads to show where to sew the dart. I'll never forget the teacher's exasperated sound when I showed her the problem. I had lifted the top layer alright, but had snipped through the material, not once, but twice!

My next challenge involved the bobbin and bobbin case. Threading the small round disc was easy and it went right into its little holder. Don't ask me how, but I managed to put that combination into the machine backwards! The teacher said she had "never in all her years" had a student do that! She worked and worked to get it out and reinserted the right way. By then I was anxious to exit her class, too.

Patterns are not limited to clothing, of course. Woodworkers use them, as do metal workers and handcrafters. Technicians use computers to create digital patterns which, at the stroke of a key, are executed flawlessly.

If only life patterns were that easy. Their results, good or bad, depend on your choices and goals. The Apostle Paul gave a big challenge when he said we should not conform to the patterns of this world. Instead, we should know and do God's good and pleasing will (Romans 12:2). It's not too hard to see the world's patterns in career goals, investments and relationships. The proof is in divorce statistics, investment scandals and murder headlines.

People who break away from worldly *me-first* patterns become nonconformist examples in a variety of ways: service to the poor, faithfulness to marriage vows, respect for people from infancy to retirement, honesty in business, and self-sacrifice for benefit of fellow man.

Good and evil both offer a variety of patterns. We can thoughtfully select the first, or deceive ourselves about the second. Patterns need adjustments for personal fit. It's a matter of discretion, so use wisdom to make your alterations and come up with something admirable. You never know who might be considering you as a pattern for living.

A CORDIAL CONNECTION

Life is pleasant when people are cordial, warmhearted and friendly. Cordiality can be shown by hospitality, generally considered a home-grown thing. I have you in my home, or you have me in yours. It sounds simple enough but we each approach it differently. Two good examples are Martha and Mary (Luke 10:38-42). Martha was overly concerned with the details of having someone over for a meal, while Mary chose to focus on Jesus and what He had to say.

Hospitality is an ancient custom that is still important today. Nomadic people were quite hospitable. If a stranger turned up at their tent door, they were expected to feed, shelter and protect them. In our society nomadic people may turn up at missions and soup kitchens. Hospitality is offered there, along with a cup of kindness to refresh both body and soul.

In English movies, like *Jane Eyre*, I'm fascinated by the hospitality shown to guests arriving at a huge estate. They were welcome to stay for weeks in rooms prepared by the staff, and cooks made sure food was served in abundance. Lovely gardens, reading rooms and horseback riding were available to fill their days; however, guests were expected to help provide nightly entertainment.

In spite of small homes and no servants, old west ranchers and settlers with barely enough to feed their own families did not shrink back. Strangers were welcome to share the beans and cornbread or a kettle of soup and homemade biscuits.

There was a time when I had a large home and a huge antique table with matching chairs. I enjoyed inviting twelve or fourteen people over for Sunday lunch. The menu never varied, only the crowd changed. I tried to invite people who did not know each other and as they got acquainted, so did I.

I live in a small home now. My table seats four and my meals have gotten simpler. Not everyone would be comfortable with our higher table and chairs; however, since the goal of hospitality is to connect with people, it doesn't have to be at home.

In our modern world, I think taking someone out to eat is a generous form of hospitality. I see three positives to that scenario. First, it allows you to focus on your guests. Second, you give of yourself as you pay the bill. Third, fellowship over some type of food, no matter what or where, provides valuable time for personal connections.

Jesus was very hospitable. For example, when the disciples would have sent people home hungry after they had sat on a hillside listening to Jesus teach all day, He miraculously made sure the crowd was fed (Matthew 14:13-21).

He also shared meals with his disciples many times, but at their last meal together He used the bread and wine to institute a sacrament we call *Communion* (Luke 22:7-20). Christians to this day follow Jesus' instructions to eat the bread and drink the cup in His remembrance until He returns (1 Corinthians 11:23-26).

Since hospitality is shown by a friendly or solicitous attitude toward people don't hold back, no matter how meager the fare. The key is to offer it cheerfully and, according to 1 Peter 4:9, "without grumbling." If you're not in the mood, don't do it. But if you are, both you and your guests will benefit from a cordial connection.

A RESTFUL RELATIONSHIP

Do you remember school days when the teacher would lead a discussion about some poem or story? She'd ask questions like, "What did the character discover? What did the author mean by this? What new understanding did you gain by reading it?" While I enjoy literature, analysis sometimes seems a little tedious.

Today, however, I stopped to analyze a Scripture that I have read many times. Some relationships in life are what I would call "high maintenance." They seem a little one-sided and there is no sense of security. I'm always wondering when I might do something wrong and the relationship will end.

Jesus' invitation to a steady relationship caught my attention so I stopped to meditate. I've never worked with farm animals, but I've seen yoked oxen facing the same direction and pulling together. He said if we took His yoke it would be a restful relationship, which would seem quite the opposite of a high-maintenance connection.

Perhaps Jesus' words stood out because my life has been hectic lately. Maybe yours has, too. As I read Matthew 11:28-30, I journaled some responsive thoughts. Jesus words are in *italics*.

Come to me
An open invitation with no exclusions
All you who are weary
Life does tend to wear us down
And burdened

We each have life loads to carry
And I will give you rest
Rest is not just sleep
Take my yoke upon you
That requires choice, partnership, relationship
And learn from Me
One leader, one learner,
The stronger helps the weaker
For I am gentle
He doesn't push for His own way
And humble in heart
He's aware of us, it's not just all about Him
And you will find rest
A knowledgeable entity that can be found
For your souls
We know when we're burdened and when we're not
For My yoke is easy
Two can lighten the load much better than one
And My burden is light
A burden is something placed upon us,
Or something we choose to pick up.

When searching for the meaning of the Greek words for *rest*, I was surprised to find that verse twenty-eight means a change by *reversal*, while verse twenty-nine refers to more of a *refreshing pause, or intermission*. I think both would be helpful, don't you?

Who doesn't look for a break or a change when life becomes heavy and distressing? Renewed energy may come when we close our eyes to rest, but it's not sleep. That's when we close our eyes and drift off into a state without conscious thought or voluntary movement.

In a yoke, if one falls asleep it only creates a bigger burden, so Jesus is offering rest. Being yoked together means walking side by side with time to communicate while moving toward completion of our everyday goals. Jesus also helps us learn more of God so that scriptural commands are lived out in the spiritually-yoked relationship. No longer are they simply do's and don'ts for a spiritual "naughty or nice" list.

This restful relationship, like all others, will come about only by our choice, not by chance.

COCOA FOR ONE

It was winter and my husband was gone on his night job. I was alone at home, grateful to be inside, warm and cozy. Later in the evening I thought *I'd sure enjoy a cup of hot cocoa, but I don't want to get out the stuff to make it.*

Those of you who enjoy opening a packet of "hot chocolate" to mix with hot water are probably saying, "What's so hard about that?" But those who enjoy an old-fashioned cup of "hot cocoa" made from individual ingredients will know why I paused. Then I realized my true subconscious thought: *Is it worth it for one?*

Though married, I am used to being "one." We never had children, so if one of us was gone the other was alone. I made myself get used to eating out, shopping, or going to church or community events by myself. It wasn't that I was anti-social, but people were not always available. So, why the cocoa question?

I'd made it for myself plenty of times before, never thinking it would not be worth it to get out the cocoa, milk, vanilla, cinnamon, sweetener and dark chocolate squares. But this time my mind had popped the question, so I pondered while I whisked the ingredients together on the stove.

My husband and I had the pleasure of starting groups for both single adults and senior adults. We met some wonderful people and made long-term friends in each one. In initial planning, singles usually asked, "What ages will this involve?" while seniors asked, "Is this for marrieds only?"

In answer to their questions, we set guidelines for each group but I also shared what I felt was the group's purpose. In fact, we named one of them *Koinonia (koy-noh-nee-ah)*, a Greek word indicating participation in fellowship with others, such as seen in Acts 2:42.

The basic guideline was that each group was to be an interest group; however, seniors always needed a further explanation. I would say, "This group is open to both marrieds and singles. All of us couples are only one step away from being single. It could happen by death, divorce or separation." On that basis, I'm happy to report I saw a real acceptance of one another in our seniors' groups.

Jesus loved to emphasize the value of *one* in His parables. Check out chapters ten and fifteen in Luke, for example. The most famous *one* may be the Good Samaritan, but here's a thought:

> In all the continents of the world,
> And all the islands too,
> There is only one me,
> And only one you.
> So we should relax and make life fun,
> Though that may mean "Cocoa for One."

FRIENDSHIP FACTORS

You've probably heard that "a friend is a present you give yourself." I think that's true, as far as it goes, but a one-sided friendship wears down and fades away after a while. Amos 3:3 asks a good question. In the Amplified Version it says, "Do two walk together, except they make an appointment and have agreed?"

True friendship comes with a two-sided connection. While you are being a friend to have a friend, they are doing the same thing in reverse. This kind of friendship is long-lasting, the giving and receiving kind.

A friend is someone who knows your faults, but chooses to like you anyway. A friend encourages your dreams and listens to your problems. They may not have solutions, but you know they care and you feel encouraged by their concern.

A friend catches your humor and you catch theirs. Laughter is one of your bonds. So is mutual interest in hobbies, entertainment, education and spiritual things. You stay active by planning times to meet for lunch, a movie, or a cultural event, indoors or out. But a quiet telephone conversation or a quick email can also strengthen your friendship.

When traveling together you understand each other's peculiarities, like going to bed early or staying up late, reading in bed or sleeping in front of the TV. Early-to-rise can live with a sleepy-head because each is *free to be me*. Mutual daily plans are made as ideas are shared on what to do, where to go and when.

Friends generally enjoy the same types of food, but not always. Food is an easy connection since we are designed to get hungry several times a day, but a beverage will do. Even special dietary needs for one will be accommodated by the other because the value is in the friendship, not the food.

Music is another factor. You may not enjoy exactly the same songs, but you connect around a particular style of music, like Gospel, Pop, Jazz, Classical or Country.

An important friendship connector, even in my teen years, was driving safely. I did not choose friends who liked to drive fast, ride bumpers or show off and take chances. I've updated those choices to include friends who do not talk on their cell phone or text while driving.

A friend is generous with your time as well as theirs. They are not possessive. They understand when you don't have time for them because of work or family responsibilities. They are willing to wait until you can connect again. Their friendship door always says, "Open."

I once saw a coffee mug that said, "Friends are the chocolate chips in the cookie of life." Thanks to Friendship Factors, I have chocolate chips and my life is sweet.

KNOCK-KNOCK

Did you automatically respond to the title by thinking *Who's There*? If so, you may have grown up with knock-knock jokes or had a child who enjoyed telling them. If you're a good sport you play along with the repartee. Here's an example: "Knock-knock. Who's there? Orange. Orange who? Orange you glad you invited me over?"

If you're an adult, you can groan now but be prepared for more because I recently saw knock-knock jokes in a children's book with an up-to-date copyright. That means they're still popular.

Who hasn't experienced a knock on the door of their home, their office or even their car window? The basic question, regardless of time or place, is always "who's there," but a knock is ineffectual unless someone responds.

Years ago I befriended an older lady who asked me if I would drive her to a home where she had previously lived. I said I was reluctant to do so, but she was very insistent, so off we went.

When we arrived, this petite lady surprised me by knocking very loudly. A child answered the door and my friend said, "Could I come in and see your house? I used to live here."

He looked at her a while before letting us in. This became a very uncomfortable situation for me as I realized there was no parent at home, but my friend was oblivious to everything but her memories as she looked around.

I was relieved that we were gone before anyone arrived. As strange as it may seem, I see only one redeeming factor in this experience. The fact is my friend died a few weeks later and I have always believed that she knew her time was limited, though I did not.

There's nothing unusual about a person knocking at a door and waiting for someone to answer. In fact, there's a picturesque verse in Scripture where Jesus says, "Here I am! I stand at the door and knock. If anyone hears my voice and opens the door, I will come in and eat with that person, and they with me" (Revelation 3:20). His use of the word *anyone* makes this an open spiritual invitation, without barriers of any kind, whether cultural, sexual, educational or financial, but He will never break and enter.

It's good not only to know *who* is standing at your door, but *why*. Jesus explains He is not just knocking to say, "Hello." His desire is that we open our heart's door so He can come in and spend time with us. Eating together implies a deeper friendship. Have you ever had such a good time sharing your life experiences, hopes and frustrations with a friend over a meal or a cup of coffee, that life seems better and you feel refreshed?

Knock-Knock. Who's there? Jesus . . . at your heart's door, but this is no joke. Will you answer His knock or pretend you're not home?

LABELS ARE FOR PICKLES

I enjoy the taste of a good pickle and rarely meet one I don't like. A fun chore while growing up was to go to our cellar and get a jar of watermelon rind pickles or bread and butter chips. We used to cut nice big canned pickles into slices for sandwiches. Now days I can buy them already cut into slabs, just waiting to liven up a sandwich.

While living in central California we were blessed with fresh fruits and vegetables from my husband's mother. I blanched and froze appropriate items, tried my hand at canning peaches and even tried to can some pickles. A friend from southern California can tell you that my pickle-canning experience was short-lived.

About the time she arrived for a visit, I was cleaning up my kitchen. I had dropped a large glass pickle jar on my tiled counter and it broke, creating a major sticky mess. Once my kitchen was clean again, I never gave another thought to canning pickles.

I enjoy buying pickles from the store. As I look at the varieties shining through their glass jars on various shelves, I think it reminds me of going to the cellar and making my choices as a child. Now we keep a variety of pickles in the refrigerator and I have discovered that some brands really live up to their commercials. The pickle aisle is about the only place I buy labels, instead of the bargain of the week.

Labels remind me of another aspect of my childhood. You could drive by most any church in town and tell from their signage if they were Assemblies of God, Baptist, Catholic, Lutheran, Methodist . . . the list goes on.

These days it's hard to find a church label because it has become popular to name a church in more general terms. I'm sure our town is not unique in the number of non-denominational labels and *community church* names.

Psalm 133:1 says, "How good and pleasant it is when God's people live together in unity." In my youthful years, Dad put that into practice by joining the ministerial association wherever he pastored. I'd say Dad taught me that labels are for pickles, not people, because he said, "You can always find a friend that loves Jesus. They don't have to be only from your denomination."

Thanks to Dad, I have enjoyed friends with many different labels. We may have agreed to disagree about some points of doctrine, but our hearts were knit together in Christian love with God's Word as our guide for living. The Apostle Paul said, "Make every effort to keep the unity of the Spirit through the bond of peace" (Ephesians 4:3).

God has a great variety of people and cultures in His family. Don't get stuck on manmade labels and miss out on satisfying friendship and fellowship which will enrich your life.

MEMORY MAKERS

Having grown up in church, and after ministering together in churches of various sizes for over forty years, my husband and I enjoy sharing our memories from time to time. They are personal blessings just resting in the background, waiting to be called forward.

A physical place to meet is called a church whether it be a cathedral or a remodeled commercial building. But the Biblical meaning applies to a group of people who function in unity while serving God and each other. They are the *wonderful people* mentioned in a song written by Gloria Gaither. She said they thrilled her with their *happy faces, praising God in heavenly places,* and I get great joy out of that, too.

I would say the Apostle Paul had some happy memories of people in the churches he established. In Philippians 1:3-5 he said, "I thank my God every time I remember you" and "I always pray with joy because of your partnership in the gospel." You may think you never do anything special in church, but every person is a *memory maker*, even the ones who serve behind the scenes and never expect any recognition.

I enjoy remembering people who served in the churches where I grew up. I was blessed by faithful Sunday School teachers, youth sponsors, camp counselors and Vacation Bible School workers. I followed in many of their footsteps.

I was an adult when my husband and I became pastors with a ministerial staff, but we all knew the church would never have grown without the help of God and His people. Sharing His love kept us all in positive motion, making the church a place of hope, joy, peace and grace.

We met hundreds of people who loved God and functioned in unity as they used their spiritual gifts and natural abilities to serve God without fanfare in their homes, churches, and communities. Many times, like Paul, I have thanked God as I remember the spiritual, physical and emotional support of faithful people who ministered together with us.

You may never have thought of yourself as a *memory maker,* but you are. Oh, sure, not all people created happy memories, but my positive memories far outweigh any negatives. Let me tell you, doing whatever you can in a helpful way, on a daily basis, makes a big difference in this world. I'd say Bob Hope got it right whenever he sang, *Thanks for the Memories.*

THE PIN THAT OPENED DOORS

I have a happy memory tucked away in my jewelry collection. It's a small round white pin wreathed in gold, with three tiny bars attached below. It was a lapel pin, popular in the fifties. Its total length measured about one and a half inches.

That was the era when our denomination challenged its churches to meet the Gold Crown Sunday School standards. The pin is my reminder of that. Yearly faithful attendance meant you had missed no more than two Sundays. After one year you earned the pin, then at two years the gold wreath was added, and with each successive year you received a tiny bar. Local perfect attendance was easy, but vacations presented a challenge.

Our family would arrive in a town on Saturday night and mom or dad would check the phone book for church information. If that didn't work, they checked a newspaper. If still no results my mom and dad, plus my two brothers and I, would pile back in the car and scout for a church nearby. It might take more than one drive around the block to read a church sign, but we were never without a place to go on Sunday.

That little pin motivated our family to attend Sunday School, but many times we opted to stay for church. Denominations differed, but I felt at home as we sang hymns, prayed, received tithes and offerings and listened to a sermon. I was even used to having the pastor shake hands as we exited the building. The commonality of worship felt homey, regardless of setting.

When my husband and I married, we decided to continue the vacation church tradition. I especially remember trying to find a church in a small New Mexico town in the seventies. I had on a pantsuit and we knew not all churches were open to that. We didn't want to offend anyone so, not finding information in a phone book or newspaper, we located three churches by driving the area. The next morning as we checked them out, we saw one with women dressed in pantsuits, so we parked the car and joined the crowd.

Inside there was a friendly atmosphere and it was easy to enter into worship along with our Christian brothers and sisters. Though we were unknown to each other, the Spirit of the Lord was there and He was the unifying factor. We have experienced this same type of unity in a wide variety of places. I couldn't name them all, but we have enjoyed worshiping in national parks, RV parks, home groups, country churches and city cathedrals.

I see a laissez faire attitude toward church attendance today that would preclude any pin program as motivation. The Bible still says, "Let us not neglect our meeting together, as some people do" (Hebrews 10:25, NLT). It would be easy to sleep in and forget the whole thing, but I come away refreshed and encouraged each time I persevere. I'm sure the creators of that pin had no idea it would open so many doors, but I'm glad it did.

THE PROMISE OF "T"

A major challenge took place the last six weeks of my Junior year of high school when we moved from the Midwest to Phoenix, Arizona. Growing up in small towns had meant that I was well-known. It also meant I walked to and from school, including a quick walk home for lunch at noon.

In the big city I had to ride a bus to school, and the fact that nobody knew me was reinforced by having to know my student ID number at all times. Besides that, I had to stay on campus for lunch. I found these changes stressful, but there was a comforting bright spot every afternoon—Mom and her tea.

Though she was a co-worker with Dad in all their pastorates, I remember years of coming home from school to find her sitting at the kitchen table with a hot cup of tea. If I walked in and she happened to be gone, I was always disappointed. I looked forward to her smile and calm demeanor. Proverbs 15:30 in the New Living Translation (NLT) says, "A cheerful look brings joy to the heart . . ." and that was Mom as she asked, "How was your day?"

It wasn't that we talked for a long time, but as we talked she made my day seem worthwhile. Proverbs 12:25 says, "Anxiety weighs down the heart, but a kind word cheers it up." Maybe I had felt like a dot in the cultural sea of education and city life, but at home I mattered. Mom took time for me.

If I thought it was hard to make friends in the last six weeks of my Junior year, it didn't get much better as a full-year Senior. In a smaller private school, many of the students had been together for years, so I ended up becoming friends with two or three newcomers like me. Though school friends were a challenge, I was grateful for the friends I made in our small, but very active, church youth group.

It was easy to catch the city bus on the corner by my home, but then life became complicated. The bus could not simply continue another mile up the street, turn left and continue about fifty-blocks to my school. It had to return to downtown Phoenix and change its route. That not only lengthened my ride, but as a small-town girl I found the noisy, dirty, over-crowded heart of the city a disturbing part of my day. Gradually, however, I did acclimate to big-city life.

I never had children so I did not have a chance to practice tea-time with a daughter, but over the years I have tried to keep up the "T" tradition. To me, "T" means TIME, not TEA. Which human being does not need some exclusive time to be encouraged or appreciated? I've heard debates on *quality time* vs. *quantity time,* but to me that's not the issue. Just do what you can, where you can, with whom you can.

"T" can include talking, treats, trips, trails, tickets, teamwork and more. Be thoughtful. Be creative. In your world, today, there's an adult or child who could benefit from some "T" for two.

THE REST OF THE STORY

I used to enjoy hearing Paul Harvey share human interest stories on the radio. He would lead right up to an intriguing point, then say, "Page Two." He would continue with another side to the story, or behind-the-scenes information, and I was always satisfied when he closed by saying, "And now you know the rest of the story."

That closing comment reminds me of something worth sharing today. Years ago the Lord dealt with me about jumping to conclusions, which basically means making a judgment quickly without knowing all the facts. I have tried to be more careful, but here's an example I've never forgotten.

I was working in our church office when a couple came in to ask for financial help. First of all, they stood out because they came in together. Working in church offices for years, I knew women generally came in alone. In one church the pastor did his own survey of men waiting out in the car, till one day he was so upset by it that he went out and told the man, "If you want help, get out of the car and come in and ask for it yourself!" I don't remember the ending, but I never forgot the incident.

I talked to this couple and we helped them out. I invited them to church and they came. As we became better acquainted, I had the privilege of mentoring the wife spiritually. I learned that they had not always been homeless. They had enjoyed a good life up north where he had been a contractor and they had actually built their dream home.

Page Two! The house burned down and they lost everything. She said, "I just never had the heart to start over." Now I knew *the rest of the story.*

When the Lord cautioned me about jumping to conclusions, the wisdom of John 7:24 seemed applicable. It says, "Stop judging by mere appearances, but instead judge correctly." Appearances are only one side of the story and I'm sure I'm not the only one aware that every story has two sides.

Another reason for caution is that Jesus said whatever measure we use to judge others will be used to judge us (Matthew 7:1-2). Do we want others to see a few things and jump to a conclusion about us without learning more about our situation?

I remember a young man telling me something years ago, when I jumped to a conclusion and shot off a reply. I'll never forget how he looked at me and said, "It must feel good to always be right." Ouch! My judgment was faulty. I had not taken time to hear the rest of his story.

I'd love to say I'm no longer a jumper, but the fact is I still have to remind myself that jumping to conclusions is dangerous. I now try to hold my opinion to myself until I can learn *the rest of the story.* It's a simple, but effective, safety net.

CHAPTER FIVE

NEVER GIVE UP

HOPE

I was thinking the other day of the first house I remember living in as a child. There was a plaque on the wall that has appeared in many antique malls. It was made of composite materials in brown tones, perhaps no bigger than eight inches by four inches, with a small tab on the back for hanging. This forties-style plaque presented only three words: ***Prayer Changes Things***.

That timeless phrase has brought hope to every generation and it's been marketed in a variety of ways. Consider each word separately and you come up with this: *Prayer*---talking to God, *Changes*---makes a difference, *Things*---circumstances, timing, relationships, and more.

I believe in prayer. I have seen changes in troublesome circumstances after prayer. Sometimes answers have come quickly, but sometimes I have had to *hang in there* a while.

HOPE! Now there's a word worth keeping in your vocabulary. Formally described, it is desire accompanied by expectation. Hope is a dynamic, energetic word. People with hope never give up because they have learned ***How Often Prayer Enables***.

Enable is a stronger word than empower. Prayer that enables provides the means, power or authority to do something or to get it done. That kind of prayer changes things! So, how often can you, or should you, pray?

First Thessalonians 5:17 says, "pray continually," so there is no limit on time and no certain place to talk to God. The Psalmist David wrote, "To you, O Lord, I lift up my soul . . . no one whose hope is in you will ever be put to shame . . . my hope is in you" (Psalm 25:1-3, 21).

Because God is greater than I am, I have hope! Because I have hope, I pray. I pray because I believe God hears me, no matter how long or short the prayer. Peter lost his faith while walking on the water to Jesus and his prayer was short. He cried, "Lord, save me!" and Jesus responded immediately (Matthew 14:25-33).

Even if our hope feels as weak and small as that famous mustard seed mentioned in Matthew 17:20, it's still powerful. A father brought his son to Jesus and said, ". . . if you can do anything, take pity on us and help us." Jesus replied, "IF . . .? Everything is possible for one who believes." The boy's father said, "I do believe; help me overcome my unbelief!" Jesus responded by healing the son (Mark 9:17-24).

HOPE motivates us to action and *How Often Prayer Enables*. I have a prayer journal with a record of one hundred sixty-eight answers to prayer in the past eleven months People of all ages, and for different reasons, would agree it's more than a motto: *Prayer Changes Things.*

I'M ALL IN

Have you ever had someone come up with a plan that would require commitment on your part? Perhaps it was a camping trip, and your friend, excited and full of enthusiasm, shared his plans. Then he asked, "Are you in?"

You don't have to be, but you decide you want to be so you say, "Yes, I'm all in." Your friend then includes you in further planning and it becomes a cooperative adventure.

You work together to bring plans to life. At the camp site you set up the tent trailer, pull out the ice chest full of food, throw a plastic cloth over the rough picnic table and set out the camp stove in an appropriate spot.

Now it's time for personal choices. You can fish, kayak, hike, rest in the rig or read in the over-size camp chairs. Just as you decide to sit down and read you notice a disturbing sight and ask yourself, "How did we miss that anthill under the table?"

The trip's initial excitement is over and some other challenging things come to mind. How far will we have to go for firewood to enjoy a campfire? Who knows how to handle this brand new camp stove? You deal with challenges one at a time and soon it is dark.

Your friend takes one end of the rig and you take the other. Snuggled in a sleeping bag, you choose to leave the tent flaps open so you can enjoy the breeze. Wait! There's a sound in the trees, a fluttering of wings. You look out but all is quiet. Then you freeze as you notice a small bear with his paws on the picnic table. You hold your breath while he sniffs the air. As he moves on, you relax. Your friend seems to sleep soundly, but you twist and turn, wishing the night would soon end.

The sun comes up and after breakfast your friend says, "I'm leaving on a hike alone, but take this." He hands you a map and points to a path at the edge of the woods. "Start over there, follow this map and I promise you'll find a most heavenly view!" Since he is an experienced guide and you have never known him to lie, you head off with faith in his words and the map.

The day gets hotter, your lunch is gone and your water has run out. How much further is that heavenly view? You check the map again, reminding yourself to stay focused. He didn't give you a time frame. He just promised you would get there.

You breathe hard as you climb one more hill and then you stop in wonder at the breath-taking view! Your friend was right when he told you the hike would be very worthwhile. There is no need to hurry, so you sit down on the ground to enjoy the encompassing view.

Choosing to be *all in* as a believer does not mean a life without challenges. It means hiking life's adventurous trail and facing its risks and unknown challenges with faith and courage. Like the psalmist David, we know God, who invited us on this adventure with Him, can be counted on for instruction, guidance and watchful care (Psalm 32:8, 62:8). We're not the only ones who are *all in.* God is, too.

KEEP LOOKING UP

Sometimes we notice a lot of jet streams in our clear blue skies. They are fascinating because we can't see the jets, just the streams trailing in their wake.

I once worked at a Christian company where employees could voluntarily attend a weekly devotional. One person each week would share a Scripture and life application. I was inspired to share Psalm 23:6 in the King James Version which says, "Surely goodness and mercy shall follow me all the days of my life . . ." Other translations mention mercy as *kindness* and *love,* but no matter which translation you read, you are being followed by two positive forces.

When I first studied that verse I thought, w*hy would these two desirable things follow me? I would prefer them to go before me.* It was then that the picture of a high-flying plane with flowing white jet streams came to mind. I understood that God in His power is carrying me through life every day. His goodness and mercy do their work on my behalf, then flow behind in visible ways to show He was there all the time. God is always at work for good in our lives, but we don't always realize it until we look back and observe the jet streams.

His power carried me through hard places in my life many times. I was sick and got well. I needed money for food and it was provided. I needed a job and got one. I desired a Christian husband and just the right man became interested in me. At the time of my prayer, only the needs were obvious. But when God went to work and answered that prayer, jet streams showed up. I could see that God had been at work in my life all along.

Our associate pastor shared an interesting thought regarding a request from Moses to see God's glory. God replied, "I will cause all my goodness to pass in front of you . . . I will have mercy on whom I will have mercy . . . but, you cannot see my face" (Exodus 33:18-23). He then put Moses in a protected place until He passed by and Moses was allowed to see God's back.

The pastor explained that the Hebrew word for *back* means *what has been.* Strong's Concordance explains it in similar fashion as *the afterward,* or *what is behind.* We may not see God's face but we know when He has been at work in our life. The *afterward* makes it easy to praise Him.

Sometimes, while looking at what is behind, we see clearly God's goodness and mercy toward us. God helped us through the test and in the jet streams of His provision, our testimony flows.

If you think jet streams of goodness and mercy have been missing from your life, try meditating on Psalm 103, one verse at a time. You might be surprised at things which remind you, "God was here!" Keep looking up. Enjoy your jet-stream view.

SHREDDED FAITH

When we first retired I had the privilege of visiting the Contemporary Arts Center in Mesa, Arizona. It was filled with artistic works in a wide variety of materials, but a creative piece by Ann Morten (2009) titled *Losing Our Shirt* really inspired my thoughts.

Ann had taken a food service worker's red shirt and punched out star shapes to shred it. There it hung, full of holes with all the star shapes scattered on the floor beneath it. You could recognize it for the shirt it had been, but there was inspiring beauty in its altered condition. By keeping all the pieces with the shirt, instead of discarding them, I saw a new and challenging message.

To me it meant *hanging in there* even when my faith may seem tattered and shredded. Faith, in any degree, carries with it a spiritual beauty. God, the author and finisher of our faith, cares about all the pieces of our life. No matter how shredded we may feel, an active faith can empower us.

Faith helps us look beyond our circumstances to the promises of God which give us hope for changes needed in things beyond our control. To *fight the good fight of faith* is to hang on to what we believe, regardless of anything that tries to convince us otherwise. In fact, the King James Version of Hebrews 11:1 identifies faith as *the substance of things hoped for, the evidence of things not seen.* The Message Bible, in more contemporary language, indicates faith is trust in God which gives us a firm foundation in life, *a handle on what we can't see.*

I'd say faith is an everyday thing. For example, we feed our body, believing it will properly sort and retain nutrients but eliminate the waste. It takes faith to pursue marriage, believing it to be a worthwhile endeavor though it is filled with unknown challenges. By faith we pursue college and technical schools to get degrees and certificates, believing they will be worth the physical, mental and financial challenges along the way.

Perhaps the psalmist's faith felt a little shredded when he wrote, "My flesh and my heart may fail, but God is the strength of my heart and my portion forever" (Psalm 73:26). The beauty of that verse is the balance. He was not afraid to be realistic about his life, but he was not giving up either. By faith he declared God would be in his life forever. That's a long, long time. How much time are we willing to give God to work in our life?

WESTWARD HO!

I enjoy living in a town that revels in its historic roots. Museums offer cowboy history and western art, Indian artifacts and pioneer buildings. A massive tree in the courthouse square has a memorial plaque stating that it was planted in nineteen twelve, the year Arizona progressed from territorial status to statehood

Visit our library and you may see an old photo, along with a letter written by a group of women who pursued a dream of free books while the town was still small and had mud streets. With hope they looked to the future and we are still reaping the benefits.

When my husband and I drive to southern California, we like to go the back way. That means starting our trip on a two-lane highway through beautiful Skull Valley with its rolling hills and ranches, then driving through small towns like Yarnell, Congress and Salome.

Out in the middle of nowhere, we always look forward to a tiny place called "Hope." A large sign proudly states, "You Are Now Entering Hope," but don't blink or you'll miss it! I'd love to meet the positive person who named that place.

We think the eight-hour drive to California feels long while driving over the desert in an air-conditioned car, but journeying over a trail in a covered wagon must have seemed endless. Our hope of visiting friends and family keeps us going, but pioneers had dreams and goals which propelled them daily from the known to the unknown.

I like the practical explanation of hope in Romans 8:24-25 which says, ". . . hope that is seen is no hope at all. Who hopes for what they already have? But if we hope for what we do not yet have, we wait for it patiently." Wagon trains contained many different personalities, dreams and abilities but they had one thing in common, a wait fueled by hope. That four-letter word persisted in moving them forward and formulated patience to help them reach their goals.

My mother-in-law, Hope, was a lovely Christian woman who lived up to her name. As a young mother, she contracted polio and was in an iron lung. Told she would never walk again, she finally recovered enough to walk with braces but hope burned strong in her heart. She wanted to walk freely. When I met her years later, she did not even use a cane and I was surprised to hear her story. Her strong faith and hope are expressed in Psalm 71:14, which in the New American Standard translation says, "As for me, I will hope continually, and will praise Thee yet more and more."

Though it may seem no stronger than a whisper inside us, hope is packed with power and creates a never-give-up attitude when we take it to heart. If you are wandering around in some wide unknown spaces, grab on to hope and inwardly shout, *Westward Ho!* Its modern translation? *Let's move forward with hope!*

WHEN THE WIND BLOWS

I always smile when I look at a photo posted in front of my desk. I took it on a vacation while trying to keep my balance by leaning against a tree. The wind nearly bowled me over as I was standing on a bluff overlooking a small valley. I finally decided to enjoy the view from our car, though there was a wire fence in that area.

I thought the fence would hinder my view but I had some great entertainment. A variety of birds did touch-and-go landings on the fence just to the right of my passenger-side window. With such a strong wind I was amazed they chose to land on a wire at all.

Finally, a pretty blue bird with a white underbelly landed with his feet about two inches apart. His tail stuck nearly straight up for balance. My photo is a little blurry because I hurried to get the picture. I thought he would take off quickly like the others, but he didn't. My husband and I both admired this little bird's tenacity since he was fighting the same wind we had just fought.

You've probably heard about *winds of adversity*. Adversity can be something physical or mental that causes us to struggle. It may cause us to feel perplexed, confused, or uncertain and we feel at a loss, wondering what to do.

In Psalm 42:5 David asked himself, *Why, my soul, are you downcast? Why so disturbed within me?* In 2 Corinthians 4:8, Paul wrote about being hard-pressed, perplexed, persecuted and struck down. Those are good reasons to be downcast, but both men chose to keep their focus beyond life's challenges and frustrations.

David encouraged himself with a little self-talk saying, "Put your hope in God for I will yet praise Him, my Savior and my God" (Psalm 42:5). Paul wrote that in spite of all the adversity he experienced, he was not crushed or in despair, nor did he feel abandoned or destroyed. He chose to focus on things unseen, "since what is seen is temporary, but what is unseen is eternal" (2 Corinthians 4:16-18).

As I watched that little bird hang on to the wire, I wondered *what's your motivation? All the other birds barely landed before they took off!* One thing for sure, it was a personal choice.

I can say from experience that supportive family and friends can be around for hours, days, and weeks on end when we are facing adversity, but at some point we are faced with a personal choice.

Like the little bird, we do a balancing act. While acknowledging the reality of what our senses tell us is happening, we can move past that to focus on eternal, unseen things known by faith and hope in God and His word. Remember, *when the wind blows* and you're facing adversity, choose your focus and hang on.

CHAPTER SIX

TIME MATTERS

A CHOICE IN TIME

The contrast between sunshine and shadow is what makes life interesting. I remember driving home from town one day in the Arizona desert when small clouds made polka dot shadows on the treeless mountains. I did not have my camera with me, but I still enjoy the memory of that beautiful moment.

Memories are part of our human composition. Everything we do creates a memory and we don't always have control over when they want to show up and take over. In fact, people dealing with grief often burst into unplanned tears when something triggers a memory. While that is a healthy part of grief recovery, we can also choose which memories we would like to linger. I call that "A Choice in Time."

Memories come as positives and negatives. When the Israelites were crossing the desert from slavery to freedom, they focused on some happy memories which they then allowed to become negative. The story in Numbers 11:4-6 might have produced conversations like this: "Remember that free fish in Egypt? And what about all those delicious cucumbers and melons we use to enjoy? This daily manna is so unappetizing. I really miss flavoring things with leeks, onions and garlic."

Their thoughts were a long way off from the positive choices offered in Philippians 4:8. There we are instructed to think on things that are true, noble, right, pure, lovely, admirable, excellent and/or praiseworthy.

Sometimes our memories need a little help. That's where journals, diaries, or lists can be helpful. Psalm 126:3 says, "The Lord has done great things for us, and we are filled with joy."

Many times I have perused my journals, giving God thanks for what He has done. I do the same with a notebook where I list answers to prayer.

Memories are very personal. In fact, one of the interesting things about family life is the different memories siblings have of the same incident. I wrote a poem about this story to remind us that some memories are worth keeping while others are not. Enjoy the freedom to select your own *choice in time.*

A CHOICE IN TIME
By Darlis Sailors

Memories float through our minds
Like clouds in the sky
Some are dark and we hurry them on
Others are bright and we ask them to linger

Memories contain both darkness and light
We live in sunshine and shadow
Forgiveness may wipe some dark clouds away
While love brightens others like sunshine

Memories can also be bitter or better
Life becomes better by choice
We lift up our head to look for more light
And choose to move out of the shadows

Memories are colors inside our mind
We pick which ones we will keep
Joy comes with light, sadness with darkness
We choose the color that's right

BLAHS AND BLESSINGS

My birthday is one week before Christmas, not my choice but my challenge. I'm used to the Christmas rush running over my birthday. In fact, many times I've joined the stampede so I've experienced both blahs and blessings over the years.

This year I received an early blessing. A friend sent a card saying, "Your Birthday is a Time to Rejoice." Inside it said, "Celebrate the life the Lord has given you from the start. Rejoice in each new tomorrow, finding joy and happiness in your heart."

God's grace was certainly in my start. I was a four-pound ten-ounce baby who arrived a little early and survived whooping cough in my first six months. I put the card's message in my journal and started counting my blessings, but then I ran across a story I had written in December of 2012 titled "Birthday Blahs."

That was the year I had planned for several months to go visit a friend for my birthday. But when we had a major snowstorm, I thought it would be wise to avoid a long drive. Disappointment gave me the birthday blahs, but my friend understood and we agreed to visit later.

When my husband arrived home from work, he asked, "Where would you enjoy lunch?" I chose a new hamburger place in the area, about nine miles away. We walked in, placed our order and then enjoyed cracking peanuts from their shells while we waited. I told him it was part of my plan to not let birthdays get me down. I mentioned a plaque I'd kept on our wall for years: *Age is a matter of mind. If you don't mind, it doesn't matter.*

Months earlier, on a walk near the courthouse square, I had visited some art galleries. One intrigued me with a whimsical painting of an elderly gray-haired lady with a bun at the back of her neck, an old-fashioned cotton-print dress with a white apron, along with round, dark-rimmed spectacles and a big smile on her face. She held a pot of smiling flowers and all the flowers in the garden behind her had big smiles, too. The artist, Ian Russell, had titled it "Welcome Wagon."

The salesgirl informed me that the painting was based on the artist's memories of the aunt who raised him. She must have been a wonderful lady to inspire such happy memories, but it reminded me of a couple of other important basics. First, do what you love and let the happiness flow through you. Second, be a woman "clothed with strength and dignity," so you can "laugh at the days to come" (Proverbs 31:25). I could see no old-age blahs for that lady.

We had no room for a large painting, but the artist offered Giclee prints so I told my husband I'd love to have a small ceramic tile. When my birthday rolled around, he brought me that blessing and I smile every time I see it. With God's help I can laugh at the days to come. That means I must remind myself to be aware of birthday blessings and choose to ignore the blahs.

FROM FIRE TO ASHES

You've heard *where there's smoke, there's fire,* but nobody talks much about the ashes. Fires bring a lot of action, from fire trucks racing down the street to curious onlookers watching firemen handle heavy equipment while dousing flames.

Investigators will observe and sift through the remains. But why bother with ashes when it's too late to save anything? It's been proven that ashes have answers and inquiring minds want to know *how did this start? Could it have been prevented?*

I was on fire for ministry in a large church for many years. I enjoyed its variety of challenges as a leader and organizer in several departments. My personal flames were like those in the fireplace, cozy and comforting. The flames lowered from time to time but the fire never actually went out, until one night when I was at a women's event.

I was sitting by myself at a small table, looking about the room, feeling disconnected from the women and isolated from the speaker. Suddenly I thought *I'm going to the women's restroom and I'll see if anyone misses me.* I was gone for nearly twenty minutes and no one came. *So much for that idea,* I thought, n*o one cares.* I went back in, but my feelings bothered me and I tried to analyze what was wrong.

Later I learned that resentment is a sign of burnout. It's easy to get to that stage because, in our society, people are valued more for what they do than who they are. Besides, ministry that is *on fire* is exciting and draws a crowd and I wasn't the only staff member who was actively burning.

About a year later, my husband and I took a sabbatical. It was a restorative time, not at all wasted though we were not involved in any ministry or work. Restored physically, emotionally and spiritually we were once again on fire, but now I was wiser. I had sifted through my ashes and discovered what I considered one important thing to help prevent burnout: REST.

You can't have *restoration* without *rest*. Things being restored are generally out of service for a time. For people that could mean a fifteen-minute break or a power nap, a day off or a vacation—something to break the routine and bring about rejuvenation.

While dealing with the demands of life, even responsibilities we enjoy, it's easy to forget that God has always considered rest important. He modeled it in Genesis 2:2 and commanded it in Exodus 20:8-11.

Forest fires are fought with *fire breaks*. We can get lost in our modern forest of busy-ness, but let's be honest. When someone asks, "What are you doing?" isn't "nothing" the last choice on your answer list? Controlled fires do a lot of good, so how will you create that restorative break? Only YOU can prevent ashes of burnout.

LIVING THE DASH

I'm living the dash and so are you, but I doubt that you think about it much more than I do. Days come, days go and we basically do whatever needs to be done; however, I was recently reminded of a life well-lived.

At a memorial for a ninety-two-year-old lady known as *Pearl,* her brother remarked that when we die our date of birth and death are formally listed with a dash in between. He said that what the dash represents is up to us. I pondered that because I had known Pearl as both a minister's wife and friend.

Dash has several meanings, but the first that comes to mind is *a short race.* Time is just a small part of eternity and life on earth varies for all of us. Pearl's race was longer than some, but she ran it with faith all the way. On screen we were reminded that *Pearl* means *a pure heart.* The Scripture shared was Matthew 5:8, "Blessed are the pure in heart, for they will see God," a promise from the Beatitudes.

Who has ever run a race without challenges? Pearl's included being left alone as a newlywed when her husband was called to the military. He not only served, but was a POW for several years. As a minister's wife for over fifty years, she faced challenges in moving to churches of various-sized congregations, in several states. She actively enjoyed her life as a wife, mother and ministry helpmate.

Dash can also mean *a little something added.* We who knew her would call that her sense of humor. Pearl could always be counted on for a joke or humorous anecdote. It was part of her zest for living. When I sent a card to say *Thinking of You,* I always tried to include something humorous because I knew she'd enjoy that.

I have mentioned some positive dashes, but there is also a negative one. Have you ever had someone *dash your hopes or enthusiasm?* Not Pearl! She made it a point to keep her dashes on the positive side. She was an encourager. You could hear her "amen" loud and clear during the Sunday sermon. Even her handshake was encouraging as she gave you a firm grip, looked you in the eye and gave a welcoming smile.

Pearl was not a game player in relationships. She lived her life true to her own self, loving the Lord with all her heart and shaping her decisions around His Word. Having observed her way of dealing with physical challenges in her last few years, I must say that when I think *Pearl,* I think *positive.*

With no control over my date of birth or death, I'm living the dash in between. Its length is unknown to me, but Pearl's example cheers me on. I wonder . . . *is there someone who does that for you?*

NO WAITING REQUIRED

Technology has certainly changed our lives, much for the better. For example, would I like to return to using an electric typewriter? No, thank you. Even though greatly improved models could finally erase my typos, not one could come close to the fast and easy use of my computer.

People of all ages are enjoying the convenience of email, Facebook, Instagram and more. The Internet is available twenty-four/seven and, whether sending or receiving, there's no waiting required. With cell phones, laptops and tablets connecting us to our world in seconds, it's no wonder people consider it inconvenient to wait for anything. But life cannot always be fast and easy. Ask anyone who has had to wait for improved health, or someone who has had to work hard to pay off debts. Ask the children who can't wait to grow up, but wait they will. We cannot totally avoid waiting.

Scripture tells us to be prepared for the day of our Lord's return, but according to Matthew 24:36-39, only God knows the day or the hour. If it were possible for us to know, don't you think someone would have figured out a way to speed it up by now? Waiting is not easy; it's a big challenge.

James 5:7-8 says that waiting for the Lord's coming is like a farmer waiting for his land to yield its valuable crop. We all know something valuable is worth the wait. Unfortunately, many people don't see the value of patience in the waiting scenario, either spiritually or for life in general.

Another word for patience is *long-suffering.* This indicates that patience is not always easy, pleasant or convenient.

Sometimes our patience is challenged by inefficient people or time delays over which we have no control; however, there are times when we can blame our frustrations only on ourselves.

By faith we may pray, "Lord, not my will but Thine be done." But faith lives out its life by patience, a fruit of the Spirit, giving God time to answer our prayers. Although we may feel like an airplane with engines running while waiting for take-off, that wait is actually positive for both people and planes.

Patience works quietly without complaint or loss of self-control. Impatience produces anger which easily boils over into harsh words, angry faces or ugly gestures. Such negatives have no positive value and certainly don't make time go any faster.

If it's true that *patience is a virtue,* then it's worth developing as an everyday character trait. Set your heart toward patience now. I can promise you one thing. You won't have to wait long for your first challenge and self-check.

PROMISES REQUIRE TIME

In sixth grade I finally got glasses. A teacher noticed I still had trouble seeing the blackboard from the front row, so she recommended an eye exam.

The doctor said I needed bifocals. Hardly any kids I knew wore glasses and I thought bifocals were for old people! I wasn't a bit happy until I heard him say, "If you wear these now, you won't have to wear them when you're older." Getting used to bifocals was not easy, but I looked forward to the day I wouldn't need them.

I graduated from high school wearing bifocals. I completed college, got married and started teaching, still wearing bifocals. Years and years went by which were filled with work as an administrative assistant and ministry associate. I remembered the promise, but there was nothing to do but wait.

In retirement I took a photography class. I noticed people around me putting on their glasses to see close up while I was taking mine off. I thought that was strange, but then I realized I'd been taking my glasses off to read for quite a while. When I mentioned it to the doctor at my next eye exam it was a happy day. I heard him say, "You don't need bifocals. You can read without them."

The nature of a promise is that it takes time to fulfill it. If you can do something right now there is no need to promise to do it later. Jesus made a promise that He was going away to prepare a place for those who believed in Him and would return later to take them to it (John 14:2-3). He also told a story to illustrate what was to take place while He was gone.

This parable, beginning in Matthew 25:14, says that a man decided to entrust his property to his servants while he went away. Each one was given a certain amount of talents to be invested wisely. One reference I read said that a talent was worth more than a thousand dollars at the time.

This parable is a good illustration about using money wisely, but its main point is that the way we live our daily lives is an investment in our future. The master returned and called the servants into account. He did not expect all to be the same, but he did expect each one to be faithful with what they had been given.

Perhaps you feel about Jesus' return like I felt about my bifocals. I heard the promise, but years went by before it happened. There was nothing I could do to make it come sooner. Jesus, like us, is waiting for the promised day of His return, because only His Father knows the day and hour (Matthew 24:36).

Promises require time. Young people think time drags by while older folks marvel at how it flies, but time is a commodity. How we use it is part of investing our talents wisely.

CHAPTER SEVEN

WELL-BEING

A MOVIE AND MEMORIES

I went to see a movie that did a good job of intertwining stories about several characters, but one stood out to me and brought memories and unexpected tears. It was a female character who had been diagnosed with breast cancer and had no one to walk with her on that journey.

I can tell you from experience that it's a shock to be told, "You have cancer which has spread and you need treatment right away." I was moved by the loneliness of this character after her diagnosis, because I remembered how my husband had made it a priority to go with me to all my tests and appointments.

I first saw my oncologist in March of 2007. I had been diagnosed with a lump a few weeks earlier, but due to insurance mix ups, by the time I got in for treatment I also had Inflammatory Breast Cancer, which was very painful. Having both a lump and IBC is not common.

In February of 2014, I went for my normal six-month follow up with a diagnostic mammogram and ultra sound. One technician said I was a *complicated case* and the other told me I was a *difficult case.* Since radiology techs rarely express opinions, I knew I was *not an easy case*, for sure.

We all have pivotal years when life takes an unexpected turn. Mine was 2007. I had eight sessions of chemo, a modified radical mastectomy and removal of eighteen lymph nodes, plus nearly seven weeks of radiation.

When I heard the actress tell the doctor she had no one to be with her, I started to cry. I thought *God, I had my husband and I had You. You were with me in 2007, 2008, 2009 . . .* as I counted the years on my fingers, I thought *Wow, God! That's awesome! And You are not going to leave me now.*

I continued to give God thanks for placing me under the care of excellent doctors and technicians. I thanked Him for the prayers and encouraging cards from our loving congregation and from family and friends. I knew God had been with me every step of the way, keeping His promise as stated in Hebrews 13:5b, "Never will I leave you; never will I forsake you."

My husband and I agree that it was difficult to receive my cancer diagnosis. Upon first hearing it, we left the doctor's office and cried together in the car. But we had to move on. Timely decisions had to be made.

I wish I could explain the closeness of God to me during 2007. Many things have changed along life's journey, but one thing has not changed. I still find God's strength and peace by reading His Word and praying. Even though I shed some tears, I'm thankful for the movie and my corresponding memories.

FREE TO BE

One summer night my husband and I decided to go downtown for pizza. It was music night on the courthouse square, so after dinner we walked slowly down the street to a nearby bench. We could hear the music and watch people come and go, but a beautiful dog produced a very special memory that night.

We first noticed him as he trotted in front of a young couple coming our way. He was on a leash but never pulled at it. He was alert, head up and not stopping to sniff or explore. He was black, short-haired, medium-sized and carried himself almost regally. We were fascinated as they walked by, but even more so when they returned.

The couple was carrying on a conversation while each enjoyed an ice cream cone. The leash had fallen on the ground and was dragging between the dog's front legs. A lot of dogs would have run off when they found they were free, but this dog continued trotting along in front of them, alert as ever. Finally, he slowed down and took the leash in his mouth. The couple didn't notice, so he continued with his regal walk and pretty soon they were out of sight. My husband and I just looked at each other and said, "What a dog!"

Even now I'm in awe of him. When the leash was dropped, he was free to be. Obviously his training and discipline kicked in and he continued steadfast on his walk. His alertness and steady pace were delightful to observe.

I'd say this dog was more disciplined than a lot of people I know, myself included. I enjoy my pastor's sermons, small group lessons and certain ministers on TV, but that's kind of like being attached to a leash. We can enjoy a fantastic walk if we stay alert to what is being said, but the challenge comes at the end of the sermon, lesson or program when the leash is dropped and we are free to be!

The seventeenth chapter of Acts contains what I call a Biblical "Tale of Two Cities." When Paul and Silas ministered in Thessalonica there was big-time resistance to their Gospel message, but in Berea it was totally opposite. The Bereans were open-minded, but not simple-minded. Acts 17:10-12 says, ". . . they received the message with great eagerness and examined the Scriptures every day to see if what Paul said was true." This personal action is what caused them to be described as people of "noble character."

Checking the Scriptures for ourselves is like taking the leash in our mouth and continuing on our spiritual walk. If you don't know how to look things up in the Bible, it's an easy fix.

For example, let's say you want to find *Psalm 19:7*. This *reference* means that first you find the *book* of *Psalms*. Here's a tip: The books of the Bible are divided into two sections, the *Old Testament* and *New Testament*. By reading the names of the *book*s of the Bible out loud a few times, you will start to become familiar with them.

Now, look in the front of your Bible for a *table of contents*, find *Psalms* and *note the page number*. Once you have turned to that page, look for a larger and darker number for *chapter 19*. The only thing left to do after that is to look at the smaller numbers and find *verse 7*. Read it, then tell yourself, "Good job, (your name here)."

Discipline yourself to learn these steps and you'll soon be trotting along, confidently enjoying what you are seeing as you read. A person of noble character moves steadily forward whether he's on a leash or free to be.

LET NOT

A friend asked recently if I was still getting good reports on my tests and labs. I've had cancer follow up since 2007 and I'm used to this question. I said, "Yes, and I'm still praying continually for good reports on all my tests." Then I shared something another friend had said a few years back.

We were on our way to lunch when she asked me to pray for a friend of hers who was being treated for cancer. Then she said, "I know you went through cancer treatments and I suppose you are always waiting for the other shoe to drop."

The thought rather startled me but I gave my heart a quick search before I replied, "No, I have never felt that way because right from the start I believed God was with me. I also believe His Word is powerful and I chose to put my faith in Him and His Word right from the beginning of my diagnosis."

When she mentioned waiting for the other shoe to drop, I pictured someone holding a heavy man's shoe over my head. If it dropped, I was going to get hurt. I could face the reality of that, but on the other hand I felt living in fear was no way to live out my life.

One Scripture I always found encouraging was John 14:27, which in the Amplified Bible says, "Do not let your heart be troubled, neither let it be afraid—stop allowing yourselves to be agitated and disturbed; and do not permit yourselves to be fearful and intimidated and cowardly and unsettled." Nothing could be plainer, but in the face of a cancer diagnosis how could I not be troubled?

As a child I memorized the King James Version which said, "Let not your heart be troubled, neither let it be afraid." It sounded simple enough then, but now it was a big challenge. How would I respond?

The phrase *let not* has the same meaning as *permit not.* To give *permission* is to give someone the go ahead or green light to do something. I realized if I let my life be lived with a heart full of agitation, fear and intimidation I would have no one to blame but myself, so I made choices.

For example, I studied God's Word prayerfully. My question then, and even now, is, "Lord, what's in this for me?" I note Scriptures that stand out to me.

You've heard *you can't keep birds from flying over your head, but you can keep them from building a nest there.* I became aware of my thoughts and determined that negative thoughts should keep on flying. I wanted only positive thoughts in residence, including good humor and laughter.

Our life challenges may differ, but we're the same when it comes to *let not your heart be troubled.* Only you can do it for you!

LOOK FOR GOOD MEDICINE

Do you try to watch for good humor every day? I do. Proverbs 17:22 says, "A cheerful heart is good medicine." I grew up with that verse but never saw its real value until dealing with cancer. I heard many times that a positive attitude is important in fighting illness, so I decided to look for the proverbial *good medicine,* the one without debilitating side effects or medical disclaimers.

This cheerful-heart medicine is very individualized. As we self-medicate, it lightens our spirit. I have some DVDs that always make me laugh, and I never get tired of people sharing the cute things said by their kids and grandkids. But since adults do and say funny things, too, good medicine is where you find it.

People seem to like receiving free samples of medicine, so I'll give you some samples of my own. The first one came from church. I was taking sermon notes when I heard the pastor say, "Let everything that has breath praise the Lord—even if it's bad breath!"

Another one came from a thrift store where I was musing over some colorful plates with a floral motif. Without thinking, I said out loud, "I wonder if my husband would eat off these?" A lady standing nearby said, "It probably depends on what you put on 'em."

Word mix-ups are always humorous to me. My husband was telling a mutual friend that I had lost all my hair during chemo, but I went to get some "glamour shocks." Our friend looked at me and said, "What?" I said, "Don't we wish. But, no, they were Glamour Shots—the pictures." She laughed and said, "Oh, I thought there was something new out there."

And I can't let you go without one of my favorite stories from a grandma. My friend heard her grandchild call a playmate "Stupid!" She called him in and said, "You can't call somebody 'stupid.' It's not nice." He said, "I'm sorry, Memaw," and went outside to play. After a while he rushed back in wide-eyed and said, "But what if they really are?"

You don't always need full-strength, laugh-out-loud belly busters. Humor comes in smaller doses to create smiles, too. For best results, follow the *Good Medicine* directions: To be taken multiple times on a daily basis, with or without food.

PERSONAL PUZZLES

Not only do I admire the pretty pictures on puzzle boxes, I admire the people who are actually able to assemble all the pieces. I have a niece who can do puzzles of twenty-five-hundred to three thousand pieces in about four days. Every Christmas I try to find a major challenge for her and she's completed every one.

I once bought a puzzle at a thrift store to give jigsaw puzzles another chance. I emptied the pieces out on a table and started sorting. My niece had mentioned that she starts by sorting straight edges and matching colors. I followed her advice and got about three-fourths of the outer edges in place and felt pretty good about it.

I worked at the puzzle off and on for a few weeks and referred to the box cover quite often. I worked a few sections of color at a time, but I wasn't making much progress. I hate to admit it, but this puzzle only had one-hundred tiny pieces. I finally boxed it up and donated it back to the thrift store.

Instead of feeling frustrated, I decided to face up to the fact that I do like puzzles, but not the kind with pieces you can handle. I enjoy puzzles on paper, like a word search or comparison of two pictures to find the changes. I could certainly see the wisdom in Paul's statement that comparing ourselves with one another is not wise (2 Corinthians 10:12).

I began to think about people. We are all born as puzzles to ourselves, our parents and others. It takes a while to put the pieces of our understanding together.

Mary and Joseph were totally puzzled when they realized Jesus was not with them as they returned home from the Feast of the Passover in Jerusalem. They retraced their steps and finally found him in the temple, listening to the teachers and asking them questions. You can picture their relief, but they were also astonished. They asked, "Why have you treated us like this? We've been anxiously searching for you."

Jesus replied, "Why were you searching? Didn't you know I had to be in my Father's house?" They were puzzled, because they heard what He said, but did not understand (Luke 2:41-52).

In those same Scriptures, Luke wrote that Jesus returned home and grew in four basic areas of life: 1) *wisdom* or mental development, 2) *stature* or physical growth, 3) *in favor with God*, or spiritual growth, and 4) *in favor with people*, social growth.

His personal puzzle took time to put together, just as ours do. But there comes a point of maturity in every child's life when he leaves home to share his puzzle with the world.

As challenging as various puzzles might be, life can be even more perplexing. But don't give up, there's hope. Philippians 1:6 says, ". . . He who began a good work in you will carry it on to completion." God has never found a personal puzzle He could not complete or solve. If you want some help with your life's puzzle, just ask.

SEED THOUGHTS

Our world is filled with small things that make a difference, seeds for instance. Such awesome creations are hidden inside their tiny shapes.

Have you ever picked up a packet of seeds? I'm always amazed at how flat and light they feel. I know you don't need many seeds to reap enjoyment from flowers or vegetables in your yard, but commercial production requires using seeds in huge quantities. If one tiny seed of grain could journal its thoughts in such a large setting, you might read something like this:

Page One: *I am only a small seed and I feel like a tiny dot in this world. My feelings are based on my outward appearance, I know, but my importance lies on the inside, unseen but powerful. One day I will be planted, though I don't know when or where. I do know I will grow at my God-given rate and my life will make a difference.*

Page Two: *I'm still just a dot in this huge field, but I'll remain in place, growing and producing what is within me. Eventually this field will be harvested and the grain will be distributed. My life will continue in a new way, but no one will know which grain came from me.*

Page Three: *Harvest is over. This field has been plowed and my roots are resting in the sun. I lived a full life, did what I could, and even now I'm enriching this field for the seeds that will follow me. I'm still unknown, but fame was not my goal. I simply wanted to know that mine was a life well-lived.*

Which of us has not, at some time or other, felt like a dot in the sea of humanity? Day after day our world is blessed by unknown people who, like the little seed, are faithful to their jobs, their families and themselves as they live out their religious and moral principles. Like the seed, theirs is a goal of personal satisfaction, not public acclaim.

In Matthew 6:1-4 Jesus taught that we should be careful when trying to do good works or help someone. Why? Because if we do it to be noticed and get public praise, that's our reward. But if we do it quietly in such a way as not to be noticed, our Father in Heaven, who judges the motives of all hearts, will be the one to reward us.

Albert Schweitzer said, ". . . the only ones among you who will be really happy are those who have sought and found how to serve." Here is a small package of *seed thoughts*. Try planting them and see what happens.

Kind **hearts** are the **gardens**,

Kind **thoughts** are the **roots**.

Kind **words** are the **flowers**,

Kind **deeds** are the **fruits**.

Anonymous

WIND, MOON AND STARS

I enjoy cars. Not only are they good transportation, they are a badge of independence. That's why teens can hardly wait to drive and seniors rarely give it up easily. But cars are also memory makers.

My husband and I have had a lot of cars during our many years of marriage. Purchases were generally mutual decisions, but one day my husband came home with a big Buick Electra that would not even fit in our driveway, let alone our one-car garage. I was so unhappy with what I called "the boat," that he took it for a trade-in on something smaller.

Many years later, one day after my mother's burial, we were enjoying a country drive near Dad's home. As we entered a small town nearby, I noticed a Porsche 914 with sparkling pearly-white paint and a black removable top parked toward the front of a used car lot.

A few blocks later I said, "Let's go back. I saw a cute little white Porsche on a car lot. I'd love to have it." My husband was shocked! I had never asked for a car before, but my drive-by choice was like new and priced right, so we bought it.

It may sound strange, but I really didn't plan to drive that car. I had a different dream. We lived in the southern Arizona desert and what I most enjoyed about it was being outdoors after the sun went down. It was fun to eat outside in the back yard or take a walk in the neighborhood, but that little Porsche helped create some of my happiest nighttime memories.

During the day I stayed indoors as much as possible, but I always looked forward to a ride in the cooler night air. My husband has always enjoyed driving while I have preferred riding, so the combination was perfect. I'd buckle up and lean back, ready to relax and enjoy the evening wind, moon and stars. It didn't take long to get beyond the street lights and out into the desert darkness. There I could enjoy an inspiring, unobstructed view with the convertible top off and the car windows rolled down.

One night I was so excited to see *the man in the moon!* I'm sure I had seen that face before, but I felt like a little child with a big discovery. Out in the darkness, the stars seemed to twinkle especially bright. Though not familiar with the constellations, it was fun to look for them. Many times I thought of Psalm 8:3-4 which says, "When I consider your heavens, the work of your fingers, the moon and the stars, which you have set in place, what is mankind that you are mindful of them, human beings that you care for them?"

I am very thankful for the sun, but I have special memories of praising God for beauty shining in the darkness. Which of God's marvelous creations cause YOU to give Him praise?

CHAPTER EIGHT

WORD CHOICES

A GREAT FISH

In spite of my last name, I'm more of a land lover than a sailor. We went on a cruise years ago and I had a daily dose of Dramamine and wore stretchy bands with a small button that pressed on my wrist, but seasickness prevailed.

I did better in small boats on the lakes of the Midwest where Dad took us kids fishing. The fish we caught were small and full of bones, but I ate them because that was all I knew. When I had my first piece of boneless cod in a restaurant, I was thrilled and crossed lake fish off my list of preferences.

Recently I read of a fish called an *Ichthyosaur (ik-thee-o-sar)* which shared the seas of the world with other large marine creatures while dinosaurs, which we perhaps know more about, ruled on land.

This giant marine creature is described as having a body eight feet thick with several flippers, eye sockets a foot across, a tail twenty-five feet long with six-foot triangular fins at the end, vertebrae up to twelve inches in diameter, a head ten feet long with cone-shaped teeth and a long, pointed snout. Based on these measurements, scientists estimate the Ichthyosaur weighed forty tons and was sixty feet long. It could breathe air and, like modern whales, lacked gills.

I couldn't picture a fish this big, so I searched the Internet for Berlin-Ichthyosaur State Park in Nevada where a lot of these fossils were discovered. A photo of a man standing next to the head of a life-sized wall carving of an Ichthyosaur gave me some perspective.

Along with thoughts of a giant fish come thoughts of Jonah, the Old Testament prophet who experienced being in the belly of one. Children's books are generally about *Jonah and the Whale*, but I checked four Bible translations and each simply said "a great fish."

A one-hundred-foot Sulfur-Bottom Whale with a ten-to-twelve-foot-wide mouth was recorded off Cape Cod in the 1930's. Whales have enormous air storage in their nasal cavity, as well as four to six compartments in their stomach, any one of which could house a group of men. To feed, they open their mouth and speed through the water, collecting food as they go

Some people think Jonah is simply a whale of a tale, but Jonah was a real person listed by name, time and place, which separates him from parables and allegories. Jonah is known as a disobedient run-away prophet, but his story shows how a loving God *provided a great fish* to swallow him, instead of letting him drown. The same Scripture passage says that God also commanded the fish to vomit a very living Jonah back onto dry land (Jonah 1:17 and 2:10, NAS).

Whether it was one of the creatures of the sea that God had already created, or one produced in Jonah's time of need, *a great fish* is obviously in the realm of reality and not at all imaginary.

DUPED BY ONE LETTER

Reading begins with learning to say the alphabet from A to Z, then matching letters with sounds. It was fun to teach beginning readers. They were excited to see that *hat* could be changed into *cat, pat, bat, or sat*, but we couldn't stop there. We moved on to whole word patterns and then put words into simple sentences. Of course, educated people learn to connect words into longer sentences and several sentences into paragraphs. Then comprehension, or understanding and drawing meaning from what is read, becomes an important skill.

Advance as high as you want to in reading and comprehension, but one thing remains constant. There are still some words in which you can change one letter to create a different word. Words in print can be reviewed again, as necessary, but the spoken word is more of a challenge. We hear it, then it's gone.

Friendly communication doesn't generally require us to be on guard, analyzing every word. Most people don't bother to maintain close friendships with a person who twists the truth for their own profit or purposely equivocates by using ambiguous words to mislead or deceive. But it does happen and God isn't the only one who detests lying lips (Proverbs 12:22).

Years ago, while we were between ministry opportunities, the Lord provided a place for us to live but we still had bills to pay and my job would not meet our needs. As we prayed about it, my husband met with a Christian businessman regarding a temporary job that would fit his non-ministry skills.

They talked over the job requirements and my husband shared what he was looking for in the way of an hourly wage. Without further discussion the man said, "We could do that," so the job was accepted.

When my husband received less than expected on payday, he went to talk to the business owner about the discrepancy and was shocked to hear him say, "I said we COULD do that. I didn't say we WOULD do that."

Filling the gap was a challenge, but so was dealing with our attitude; we felt deceived. Anyone familiar with the Lord's Prayer knows that as we forgive those who do wrong against us, the Father in heaven also forgives our wrongs against Him (Matthew 6:9-15).

We changed bitter to better, not just by one letter, but by forgiving the man and praying over our finances. By God's grace, my husband went to work and did his best on a daily basis and the money stretched to meet all our needs.

Being duped by one letter was an experience we have never forgotten, but certainly not one we want to see repeated. The God-honoring character qualities mentioned in Psalm 15 include speaking truth from the heart. That goal is both worthy and attainable.

PUT THAT IN WRITING

Formal documents like marriage and birth certificates, deeds and titles have carried legal weight for centuries and turned up in antique stores for years. Less formally, when people ask us to "put that in writing," they are interested in simple documentation for future reference.

Paper goods are considered ephemeral because of their potential for a short life span, especially without proper storage. I had a nice box of antique calendars, valentines and greeting cards, plus old photographs, artful place mats and programs which I lost entirely when our rented storage space in western Washington leaked like a sieve during a big rain.

I used to look for ephemera such as postcards and letters at trade shows because of their informal communication. The sender considered an expression of love, a thank you, or news of a special trip important enough to put into writing. The receiver valued the message enough to save it, probably not thinking that years later a finder like me would enjoy a peek into their past.

As a child I had a favorite Bible story book, but as I got older I chose to read the Bible itself. Even in the old King James English I found it full of adventure, love, mysteries and promise.

My Bible is in modern English now, but for me the bottom line has always been the wonder of God wanting us to know Him so well that He put everything into writing. Most anyone can tell you the danger of written messages these days. Even a casual email or Facebook posting can be used against you forever.

Rest assured that God's communication was not casual. In fact, He was so purposeful in what was written that He guaranteed His Word would not return to Him empty. He said it would "accomplish what I desire and achieve the purpose for which I sent it" (Isaiah 55:11).

When reading a biography, I'm always intrigued by the author's documentation of their sources. Theologians and historians can document a lot about how the Bible was written, but its real value is its expression of God's love. We didn't even have to ask! He just put that in writing and now we can read His Word and hold Him to it. In fact, it's what He likes us to do. If you haven't done that yet, it's never too late to get started.

SHADES OF PRAISE

Have you ever tried to pick just the right shade of a desired paint color while standing in front of an overwhelming display of samples? You finally pick one card, only to see more suggestions of complimentary hues. You can become positively dizzy with color choices, but that endless variety is part of its enchanting beauty.

In painting our small retirement home, I chose very light pastel hues for each room. There was light blue in my office, light green in our bedroom/bathroom and pink to match Mom's wallpaper in the kitchen. I finished it off with a neutral shade in the living area. Using color was fun, especially as a neighbor offered to do the work and all we had to do was buy the paint.

In the days of polyester pantsuits, patchwork skirts and granny glasses we were in a church that grew because of The Jesus Movement. This spiritual phenomenon among the youth caused our congregation to grow by leaps and bounds. Love for the Lord permeated the lives of these young people and they used their unusual creativity to bless the rest of us.

Our church was situated next to a busy freeway and was highly visible. The buildings and grounds were well-kept, but one young landscaper decided it would be nice to create a big PRAISE THE LORD out of colorful flowers on a dirt bank which ran along the entrance to our property.

He went to work outlining thirteen oversize letters, plus the needed space between the three words, and the results were awesome! We church people thought it was great, but the church also received positive comments from commuters who traveled the freeway.

When plans were made to build a new and larger church next door, one of our young Christians saw the steeply-pitched roof as a great place to honor the Lord. He skillfully built up the brown shake shingles in perfect dimensions to create a beautiful cross. It could be seen as you drove down the freeway toward the church. People considered it awesome in both size and simplicity.

God appreciates both color and design. Starting in Exodus, chapter thirty-one, we can read of God's exact plans for both in the instructions given to Moses for a moveable Tabernacle to be used for worship as the people journeyed across the desert. We also read how God gifted two men, Bezalel and Oholiab, to be not only master artisans but skilled teachers, so that others could be trained to help with this special project.

Psalm 150:6 says, "Let everything that has breath praise the Lord." Two living, breathing young men chose to praise God with flowers and roofing materials and worked hard to complete their designs so others could praise the Lord along with them. There is no limit to human creativity, and there are many shades of praise that God has yet to enjoy.

WHAT'S IN A NAME?

A name like Darlis brings confusion. No one ever gets it the first time around. Most people think it's Darla. Sometimes I get tired of explaining the real spelling to people in passing, so I say, "Just add an 's'."

I always thought it would be nice to have some exotic story to share with those who ask, "Where did your name come from?" But the simple truth is that I'm not named after a family member or friend. Mom just heard the name in a store, liked it and filed it away for future reference.

To me a simple one-syllable name like Ruth or Ann would have seemed heavenly. Who could mistake those the first time around? But my theory about simplicity has been blown away repeatedly. I started giving a shortened version of my middle name at restaurants and coffee places. I would say, "Jean," and most of the time it would come out spelled *Gene*. Oh, well.

Most parents put a lot of time and thought into their child's name. You can buy books of names or research them online. Family history generally becomes part of the discussion and tiny babies can end up with some pretty hefty labels.

My suggestion is that parents try to make at least one of their names simple enough for public consumption. Think about how the child will be sharing that name in a multitude of social situations in the next sixty or seventy years.

That's what God did when He sent His Son to earth on a mission of redemption. In a dream, God sent an angel to Joseph who said a Son would be born to Mary and they were to name Him Jesus (Matthew 1:20-21). Mary received a similar message from the angel, Gabriel (Luke 1:31). Wouldn't you have loved to hear Mary and Joseph sharing how they each came up with the same name?

What's in a name? Proverbs 22:1 says, "A good name is more desirable than great riches; to be esteemed is better than silver or gold." Most people are not born with the proverbial silver spoon in their mouth. It takes time and effort to acquire riches in any great measure. The same holds true for acquiring a good name. Have you noticed the way commercials try to stress how their product can be trusted? They hope you will remember their name while you are shopping to meet your needs.

Rich name value starts building up early with things like making good choices, concern for others and speaking words that can be trusted. I was given an unusual name at birth, but it was up to me to give it desirable value.

Maybe you're thinking *nobody cares about my name*, but they do. Each name is important whether short or long, common or unusual. Just remember: The value is not in the letters, but in the living.

WORD POWER

I've been thinking of seven little words spoken by a real estate agent nearly twenty years ago. He was not a big talker but he did his job well. We didn't need all the space in the large home we had been renting, so we were looking to buy a small condo.

The housing market was tight, but we finally found a 2BD/2BA unit in a former apartment complex with older construction. This meant no sound barriers between unit walls or floors. What really surprised me was to smell cigarette smoke from the floor below when I opened the cupboard doors beneath the sink. We stuffed in some insulation, which helped, and settled in to enjoy our affordable space.

We had moved to the area with high hopes. But my husband's employment opportunity had not turned out as expected and I was working temporary jobs, which I hated. I guess my frustration must have been noticeable. We signed the papers, but not with joy. As the agent was leaving he simply said, "Things have a way of getting better." That was it . . . seven little words spoken quietly and calmly from a man we did not see again.

Words are interesting things. Even short and simple ones have inherent power. Remember chanting as a child, "Sticks and stones may break my bones, but words can never hurt me"? We didn't have to live very long to know that, though it was fun to say, in reality it was a lie. Sticks and stones may break bones and we'll recover, but hurtful words can abide inside us forever.

I've worked with both children and adults who were timid and using less than half their awesome potential because someone in their past had said, "You're stupid. You can't do anything right. Get out of the way. You don't know what you're doing!" Negative words entered through their ears into their mind and spirit, playing like a cassette tape with lifetime automatic rewind.

Don't underestimate the power of your words. It's not just *what* you say, but also *how* you say it. "You fat little baby," can sound harmless when said in a soft cooing way by a mother with smiling eyes. But the same words hold a different power when said harshly by a caregiver who is glaring at a little one in need of a diaper change.

Proverbs 16:24 in the Amplified Bible says, "Pleasant words are as a honeycomb, sweet to the mind and healing to the body." Words, like bees, have the power to both sting and make honey. Honeycombs are six-sided cumulative structures, built and filled cell by cell. From birth we are like honeycombs, holding on to what we hear from people around us. As adults we like to think that words can no longer hurt us, but let's be honest. They do.

Whether we are on the giving or receiving end, words have staying power. Sometimes we have the first word, sometimes the last. The question is, "Will it be a sharp sting or sweet honey?"

WORDS OF LIFE

I worked for several years as an administrative assistant on a large staff where I had the opportunity to attend a professional training seminar of my choice each year. One which really stuck with me taught the difference between being assertive and aggressive. It seems that aggressiveness was considered more of a male trait, but women could hold their own by learning how to be assertive.

I grew up in a peaceful environment, so aggressiveness and confrontation generally caused me to pull back. I was relieved to learn that I could be assertive without being aggressive. It took some practice to communicate something in a powerful and positive way without backing down, but that did not mean I was unwilling to compromise. I noticed that aggressive people were more ruthless, intent on their desire to dominate, whether it was a conversation or a pending decision.

I used to be amused by people's comments when they learned that I worked on a church staff. A common response was, "It must be so nice to work in a church," as if we were all angels and there was no need for basic office communication skills.

Jesus said, "Blessed are the peacemakers . . ." (Matthew 5:9), and we needed to work toward that as much as in any other work place. To be the *maker* of anything requires some effort and that's what it takes to create a compromise. People have to give up a portion of their personal goals or desires to create a win-win situation for everyone, but aggressive people tend to bog down the process. They are certain that it must be *their way or the highway,* as the old saying goes.

A couple of years ago I wrote a poem called "Words of Life." It focused on the power of pronouns. They may be small, but don't be misled. They carry a lot of weight when trying to bring two people into agreement on a *win-win* compromise.

WORDS OF LIFE
By Darlis Sailors

Words have length and words have power
Say "I" and it marks my place
The world is big, and I am in it

Say "you" and life gets larger
I admit that there are others
I have a place, but so do you

You and I can join as one
Show strength as "we," a force for change
We, as a team, produce good or evil

Alone I am one, my choice
With you, I must learn to give
Our spaces touch and new vision emerges

How will we live, part you---part me
Our plan is formed with give and take
Small words of life with power

AUTHOR'S NOTE

As a young child, Darlis would go to her father's home office and browse the encyclopedias for pictures. Her father nurtured her interest by taking her to the local Carnegie library and her appreciation of books and libraries has never waned.

She graduated from *Vanguard University* in Costa Mesa, California as an English Major with a Minor in History. As a certified teacher in that state, she taught early elementary grades before opening a music studio in her home. Her musical talents on organ and piano were used to assist church congregations as well as choirs.

Darlis has always been an active volunteer who started young as a teacher in Sunday School and Vacation Bible School. In her teens she was a youth leader. As an adult she has used her teaching skills to work with children and adults of all ages. As an administrator she has developed materials and trained leaders for various ministries, and she has had years of experience in creating and publishing weekly church bulletins and monthly newsletters. Perhaps it is this background that has led her to develop weekly inspirational stories in a short format of five hundred words or less.

At the urging of a friend, Darlis became a member of *Oregon Christian Writers* (OCW) and she continually finds their newsletters and conference materials informative and inspiring. She is also a member of *Professional Writers of Prescott* (PWP). Their monthly speakers and quarterly workshops have broadened her understanding of writing dynamics, an interest she has explored deeply since her retirement.

Darlis always enjoys movies based on true stories and events, photography, traveling with her husband, local walkabouts, and creative writing. She has notes in place for future books for adults as well as a variety of children's stories. Check out her website at AuthorDarlisSailors.com. She enjoys hearing from her readers at darlis.sailors102@yahoo.com.

CPSIA information can be obtained
at www.ICGtesting.com
Printed in the USA
FSOW03n0355010217
30139FS